HISTORY OF ROCK MUSIC

Richard T. Dasher

J. WESTON WALCH PUBLISHER

PORTLAND, MAINE

1   2   3   4   5   6   7   8   9   10

ISBN 0-8251-2676-2

Copyright © 1985, 1995
J. Weston Walch, Publisher
P. O. Box 658 • Portland, Maine 04104-0658

Printed in the United States of America

Contents

1. Introduction 1

2. Popular Music, 1900–1950 3

3. Blacks and Blues 13

4. Where the Bluegrass Grows 21

5. The Beginnings of Rock and Roll 31

6. The British Are Coming! 37

7. Surf's Up! 45

8. The Folk Movement 51

9. Etched in Acid 59

10. Soul, Memphis, Motown, and TSOP 65

11. Art Rock—Or Is It? 71

12. Jazz-Rock and Fusion 79

13. Disco, Reggae, Punk, New Wave, and Whatever 83

14. The MTV Generation 89

    Coda 97

    Glossary 99

    Bibliography 101

    Index 103

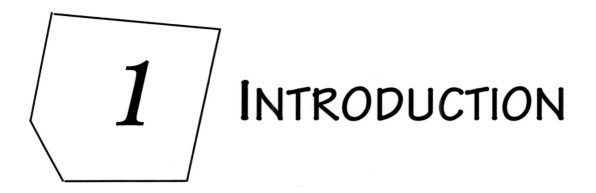

1 INTRODUCTION

TO: Trog Zaxtrax, Imperial Governor for the Thirteenth Galactic Sector.

Greetings!

Most noble Trog, I have the misfortune to inform you that I have been forced to cancel our colonization mission to Sol III and return to Digopek for reassignment. This has been made necessary by the fact that Sol III's inhabitants have somehow discovered our approach, and are bombarding our vessel with electromagnetic wave-pulses of astonishing violence. The pulses are periodic, and when converted to sound consist of forceful pounding, together with howling or wailing noises and wild electrical shriekings. I believe this weapon, which the natives call "rockaroar," or perhaps "lokenlol," is designed to shake our space vessel to pieces if we approach much closer. Our soldiers have headaches from the violence of this weapon, and the androids twitch in time to the pulses. I will report to you personally, with recordings of this awesome weapon, in six gbzots.

Hail the Emperor!

Maglev,

Commander.

In all probability, no Commander Maglev ever sent such a message. Still, one wonders what an alien race might make of the radio and television broadcasts that this planet constantly emits. Rare is the Earthling who has not been exposed to, even saturated with, rock and roll during most of his or her life. Russian teenagers listen to Russian rock groups playing and singing American songs as well as their own creations. A jukebox in Niamey, Nigeria, included "Rock Around the Clock" among its selections in the 1960s. Natives in the jungles of Sarawak were hooking electric amplifiers to a native stringed instrument called a *sapeh* at about the same time. Eskimo youngsters wear T-shirts with "AC-DC " printed on them.

Obviously, this music called rock must address something very basic in the human makeup. It somehow bridges cultures as different from each other as Alaska is different from Zaire. What is the magic that *this* music, of all the many musical "languages" and "dialects" around the world, has for so many people in so many different places?

To be truthful, we don't know some of the answers to this question, and the answers we do know aren't simple. To young East European fans, rock offers a way to show a sense of unity with the youth of the West. To Third World fans, it offers a chance to taste the lifestyle of the affluent First World of Europe and America. To West Europeans, rock is the unifying element of an international youth culture whose members share more or less common attitudes toward their respective societies. To an extent, rock means something different to each of its constituencies.

In most places, however, rock is associated with young people who live in the fast lane. Its essence is the primacy of now over later and of feeling over intellect. It speaks the language of the world's Peter Pans, people who want to remain teenagers forever. To its partisans, rock represents the freedom to try new lifestyles and to discover one's own self, rather than simply to fulfill parental expectations. Detractors view rock as the expression of depraved degenerates, the sick sludge of a permissive generation. Both views find support in rock's tendency toward romantic excess, theatrical gestures, and pompous display. The young might see Michael Jackson as a superhero, wonderfully free of mundane existence, a twitchy, beanpole analog for Spiderman. Their parents often perceive the group as tasteless, a carnival freak show that makes loud, horrid noises.

In short, rock is controversial. It always has been. From its earliest beginnings, rock has been the musical expression of adolescent rebelliousness. As parents gradually came to terms with rock, and gradually transformed it into Muzak, new and more outrageous styles of rock emerged.

Rock is also, like jazz, uniquely American. In fact, it's hard to imagine a musical idiom such as rock beginning anywhere else in the world. Where but in America could the fusion of black rhythm-and-blues and white hillbilly music take place? Who but an American, half folk artist, half gadgeteer, would create the electrically amplified guitar? True, the British have done much to alter the direction in which rock has evolved, but the *invention* of rock and roll—that was as American as shoofly pie and black-eyed peas. The *History of Rock Music* is the story of how rock was born, and grew to a ripe age.

2 POPULAR MUSIC, 1900–1950

"By the light of the silvery moon,
I want to spoon; to my honey
*I'll croon love's tune . . ."**

No question about it, such sentiments are as out-of-date as straw boaters, Gibson Girl calendars, and the Great White Fleet. This song is as appropriate a reflection of its era—the turn of the twentieth century—as was "The Camptown Races" ("doo-dah, doo-dah") of a half-century before, or as "I Want to Hold Your Hand" was of the period some sixty years later.

All three songs mentioned above were enormously successful examples of what is called popular music, each representing its specific era. Most people have a pretty clear picture of what is meant by *popular music*—songs that are widely heard and enjoyed for a limited time period, songs that express the sentiments of an era in a rather superficial way, and which fade from memory as the era passes into history. Some songs, like meteors, blaze briefly and then are quickly forgotten; how many of the Top Forty songs of two years ago do you still hear? (Indeed, how many can you remember?) Other songs, like auroras, glow and shimmer for some time; most people know "Seventy-Six Trombones," or "Maria" (from *West Side Story*), and once in a while you hear a disco version of "Begin the Beguine," or some such golden oldie.

Most popular tunes have *texts*—lyrics—just about as trite and shallow as those at the beginning of this chapter. After all, popular music is usually entertaining and relaxing, not very philosophical or profound. Once in a while a "heavy" song makes it onto the pop charts and sticks around for a while. Songs like "Send in the Clowns" are such exceptions.

---

* "By the Light of the Silvery Moon," Edward Madden and Gus Edwards, 1909.

Some popular songs are thoroughly topical, linked with some historical event. Songs like "Just Before the Battle, Mother," expressed feelings common to many Civil War soldiers, North and South. George M. Cohan caught the national mood perfectly in his World War I marching tune, "Over There." Later, Bob Dylan gave words to the sentiments of a generation in his "Blowin' in the Wind." Such songs, of course, tend to fade from popularity as soon as the events they reflect pass into history.

Minstrel Shows

Popular music has been part of European and American culture at least since the 1500s. Many of the pop tunes of former ages have worked their way into the folk music of various nations. In the 1800s, arias from operas sometimes made it to hit song status. *Operettas*, musical shows with light, romantic plots and much spoken as well as sung dialogue, provided songs for both Old World and New throughout the last century.

Beginning around 1840, a new type of entertainment arose in the United States, and with it came a new type of song. This was the *minstrel show*, a variety production featuring comic scenes, monologues, sentimental solo songs, and solo and ensemble songs of a humorous character—all presented in black-face makeup and in a faked "Negro" accent. Minstrel troupes achieved enormous popularity and retained it until well into this century. Some of the best-known popular composers of the day— Stephen Foster, Dan Emmett, James Bland, William C. Handy—were minstrel musicians.

Many of the minstrel tunes, such as Foster's "Camptown Races" and Emmett's "Dixie," were lively pieces suited to ensemble performances with banjo accompaniment. Equally common, however, were sentimental solo songs such as Foster's "Beautiful Dreamer" or James Bland's "Carry Me Back to Old Virginny." Much of the popular music of the late 1800s can be classified under one of these two broad styles. The same can be said for music today.

Beginning in the late 1890s, a new type of music rose to popularity in this country. *Ragtime* was essentially piano music, the pieces themselves structured like a military march but the syncopated right-hand figures borrowing from banjo-picking techniques. Very few rags had words set to them originally, but ragtime did have considerable influence on the pop songs of the period, for raggy melodies and accompaniments were the rage. Tunes such as Joe Howard's "Hello, Ma Baby" and Hughie Cannon's classic "Bill Bailey, Won't You Please Come Home" evoked the spirit, if not the actual technique, of the piano rag. By 1911, when Irving Berlin wrote "Alexander's Ragtime Band," the jittering, toe-tapping infection of syncopation was epidemic.

Operettas and Musicals

Of course, there *were* other styles of popular music at the time. The operetta was the equivalent of the Broadway show in that period. The versatile cellist, conductor, composer, and businessman Victor Herbert wrote his first operetta in 1893, and his first smash hit (*The Fortune Teller*) in 1898. Over the next twelve years, a series of enormously popular shows—*Babes in Toyland, Mlle. Modiste, The Red Mill, Naughty Marietta*, to mention a few—poured from his prolific pen. The light, carefree ballads and waltzes reveal Herbert's European training in every line and lilt.

Less graceful but more distinctly American were the brash, strutting songs of George M. Cohan. A song-and-dance vaudevillian from childhood, Cohan specialized in playing the cocky, flag-waving shrimp. His nearly autobiographical song, "I'm a Yankee Doodle Dandy," was composed for himself to perform in the show, *Little Johnny Jones*—written by (who else) George M. Cohan. This was followed by "You're a Grand Old Flag," and ultimately by the song that earned him a Congressional Medal of Honor, "Over There." Cohan's talents were not exclusively reserved for superpatriotic songs, though. This Jewish boy from Rhode Island wrote one of the most characteristic statements of Irish pride in his song, "Harrigan." In addition, his "Mary's a Grand Old Name" is a lovely and touching celebration of straightforward simplicity.

Cohan's direct and charmingly naive tunes echoed the unsophisticated songs of the 1800s. But even as he wrote, another generation of Tin Pan Alley composers were evolving a new, more subtle, and worldly type of song. Three years after Irving Berlin wrote his wildly successful song, "Alexander's Ragtime Band," a newcomer named Jerome Kern wrote a show, *The Girl from Utah*, which contained the haunting ballad, "They Didn't Believe Me." Earthier than the Victor Herbert confections, and much subtler than Cohan's typical cheerleading tunes, this ballad marked the appearance of America's classic era of popular music. Kern continued over the next thirty years to write an amazing variety of superb songs, and probably the most influential and important musical of all time, *Showboat*. This work changed forever the way musicals would be written. Kern eliminated the dancing girls and the variety-show structure of the typical musical, focused on character development and moving the plot along, and (most daring of all) addressed the inequities of racial prejudice in this landmark show (1927).

From the late 1930s onward, Kern's songs expanded the musical craft with which popular tunes were written. "All the Things You Are," for example, is a marvel of chromatic harmonies. "Long Ago and Far Away" has a second phrase that rockets away into a remote key (of the lowered third) before returning home for the third phrase. "All Through the Day" uses this same key relationship in the last phrase, where the change of tonal center is used to highlight the change in words from day to night.

Finally, Kern's place in pop-song history could have been made secure by only one song, written as World War II broke like a fearful storm over Europe. "The Last Time I Saw Paris" is a simple song, gentle in sentiment, folklike in character. It so perfectly expressed the feelings of so many that it became associated with the wartime period much as "Over There" had reflected the nation's attitude during the First World War.

Perhaps the most perfect matching of words to melody occurred in the works of Cole Porter. Always sophisticated and tasteful, even in his uninhibited celebrations of sex ("Let's Do It," "Love for Sale"), Porter's songs matched the best output of Jerome Kern. Songs like "Night and Day," "Begin the Beguine," "What Is This Thing Called Love?" and "In the Still of the Night" were musical landmarks of their era.

The list of other excellent writers of popular songs in the 1930s and 1940s could easily be extended to book length. The composers and tunes mentioned here may serve as a small sampling of the best of an era. No list of the songwriters of the period could be representative, however, without mentioning Richard Rodgers and his two best-known lyricists, Lorenz Hart and Oscar Hammerstein. Like the composers mentioned previously, Rodgers was best known for his musical shows. His facility at tapping a spring of flowing melody is illustrated by the fact that he tossed off the song "Bali Hai" (from *South Pacific*) in five minutes over a cup of coffee. Where a list of songs can represent, say, Cole Porter, it is easier to list the outstanding musicals of Richard Rodgers—*Oklahoma!*, *South Pacific*, *Carousel*, *The King and I*, and *The Sound of Music*, to touch only the peaks.

Jazz and the Swing Bands

One did not have to attend the theater to hear popular music in the early years of the century, however. At the beginning of the century, the market for pop songs was the sheet music trade, since the phonograph was a crude and scratchy device, and radio was in its infancy. Many people played the piano well enough to thump out the latest song by, say, Rudolph Friml. If your own pianistic skills were limited, you could buy a player piano and get piano rolls of your favorite pieces. If you weren't sure of your ability to play the latest tune, you could go to a music store and listen to the music "demonstrator," a competent pianist who would play through a song you were considering.

By 1915, the technology of sound recording and playback had progressed to the point where you could at least recognize the song on the record. Recording was still done acoustically; one had to shout or play into an immense horn, which scratched a groove in the wax by brute force. In 1917, when the first jazz recording was made, this crude process was still the best that was available. It wasn't until the late 1920s, in fact, that a better electrical process, using microphones and an electrically driven recording needle, came into general use.

The early radios also left much to be desired. For several years, crystal sets, with "catwhiskers" and tuning coils, were the only equipment available. Only one person could listen at a time, since they had earphones in place of speakers. Eventually, tube sets replaced the crystals, and the family could sit around the radio and listen to their favorite shows. Only on calm nights, though; the sets were all tuned to the AM frequencies, and a thunderstorm would mar the reception with loud bursts of static.

By 1930, then, one could buy comparatively decent-quality recordings, or could listen to recordings or live performances on the radio. One could hear the Paul Whiteman or Ben Pollack bands from New York, or perhaps the Louis Armstrong Hot Five or the Lang-Venuti All-Stars from Chicago, or the Casa Loma Orchestra from Toronto. Some groups had regular weekly shows, to which their fans listened faithfully. Besides that, you could go down to the drugstore and sip a malted and put nickels in the jukebox to hear your favorites again. Since that was the beginning of the Great Depression, you might want to listen to the new pop singer, Bing Crosby, singing "Brother, Can You Spare a Dime?"

The early 1930s were hard times in the music business, just as they were in most businesses. However, by 1935, the national mood was changing, and with a famous radio broadcast from Hollywood, California, Benny Goodman's band launched the *swing* era, which held sway over popular musical tastes right up until the middle 1950s. This was indeed a golden age for popular music, for the superb songs of Tin Pan Alley's finest were performed in rhythmic, sophisticated arrangements by excellent musicians. Bands fronted by leaders such as Tommy Dorsey, Glenn Miller, Benny Goodman, and a hundred others, were solid musical ensembles with something distinctive to contribute to the musical world. Add to that the solid jazz of Count Basie, the splendid quality of the Ellington band, the tight, swinging ensemble of John Kirby, and the *joie de vivre* of Cab Calloway, and you have described a classic era of popular music.

The sound of big swing bands dominated the airwaves, but there were other kinds of popular music as well. In the 1920s, ragtime gave way to a new piano style, called *stride* piano because of the actions of the player's left hand. On the first beat of a measure, the left hand would play a bass note; then on beat two, it would play a chord an octave or so higher. Beats three and four repeated the pattern, resulting in a bass-chord-bass-chord accompaniment for the melody:

This was not so new; ragtime had almost the same left-hand pattern. But now the keys were played gently, almost caressed, rather than being thumped firmly as in the "boom-chuck" style of the rags. Sometimes the stride style was varied by a "walking bass" or a passage of parallel tenths:

Stride piano—as played by Earl Hines, Fats Waller, Art Tatum, or Teddy Wilson—became the standard fashion for informal, popular piano playing. However, no sooner had it become the fashion than still another piano style emerged and, for a few years, became the rage much as ragtime had done before it. This was the rhythmic, driving, blues-based idiom called *boogie-woogie*. The heavy left-hand ostinato gave a raw energy to this music that young people found irresistible. Performers like Mead Lux Lewis, Pete Johnson, and his smooth, elegant partner, Albert Ammons, acquired national fame for a short while.

The high point of the swing era occurred just before World War II, in the works of the bands of 1940 and 1941. The major swing bands played show tunes and popular songs, but they also played a repertoire of specials that were associated with one particular band. Whenever you heard the tune "Marie," for instance, you knew it had to be the Tommy Dorsey band. "Let's Dance" was Benny Goodman's theme. The Glenn Miller Orchestra recorded lots of specials, "Moonlight Serenade," "String of Pearls," "In the Mood," and "Pennsylvania 6-5000" among them.

America's entry into the war put the development of popular music on ice for the duration. Some bandsmen joined the services as musicians, some served in other branches; some stayed home and played for USO shows, keeping civilian morale high. When the war ended in 1945, many people tried to pick up where popular music had left off in 1941. The bloom was gone, though, and most of the bands suffered from overweight. Dorsey's group had lost much of its bite, and added a small orchestra of strings for a lush sound. Many of the other groups followed the same path. Popular groups cast about for a new sound that would catch on—lush strings and celeste behind Doris Day, or three French horns and rhythm, or some other reworking of the basic sound of swing. What the world needed was a new type of popular music. When it finally arrived, that new sound came from an unexpected—and, to some, a most unwelcome—direction.

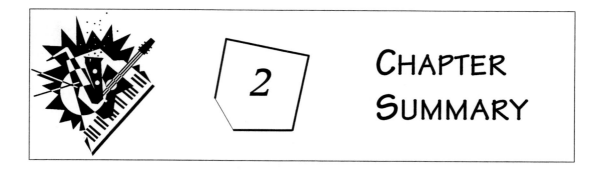

2 CHAPTER SUMMARY

America has had a distinctive popular-music style since the advent of the minstrel show in 1840. Since that time, our country has created many kinds of music—ragtime, jazz, blues, swing, boogie-woogie—that were originated by black Americans. Certain other popular song types, such as ballads and the music of operettas and Broadway musicals, have been mostly of white American inspiration. The two styles, black and white, traded ideas back and forth freely, and with each generation they found more and more common ground with each other. "White" music has become more black-influenced, and "black" music has evolved toward the white style. By the end of the swing era, it was obvious that a true synthesis of the two would be just a matter of time.

Suggested Projects

1. Make an oral history of the swing era. Talk to your parents or grandparents who lived through the Second World War. Ask them about the popular music then, as well as the dances and the personalities that were nationally known. Write a report based on your research.

2. How many recordings can you find of songs from the first fifty years of this century? How many rereleases of original pressings can you find? How about original recordings themselves—old 78-rpm discs? Be careful with them; they are fragile and may be worth something to collectors. Play some of these songs for the class and discuss the style.

3. This chapter has mentioned a number of personalities of the era—Victor Herbert, George Cohan, Paul Whiteman, Duke Ellington, Glenn Miller, and so on. Many of these people had fascinating lives; one, at least, even had a mysterious death. Select five of them and report on their careers.

Suggested Books

Ewen, David. *Panorama of American Popular Music.* Englewood Cliffs, NJ: Prentice-Hall, 1957. This work, by one of the foremost reseachers in American popular music, contains good, short chapters on minstrelsy, operettas, Tin Pan Alley, musical comedy, and prominent personalities. It also contains brief notes on the swing era.

Keepnews, Orrin, and Bill Grauer, Jr. *A Pictorial History of Jazz.* New York: Crown Publishers, Inc., 1966. Contains seldom-seen photos of swing bands and their leaders.

Spaeth, Sigmund. *A History of Popular Music in America.* New York: Random House, 1948. Scholarly, detailed discussions of the music of all periods up to 1948.

Walker, Leo. *The Wonderful Era of the Great Dance Bands.* Berkeley, CA: Howell-North Books, 1964. Contains some fine shots of various bands, major and minor, including some late-1940s pictures of bands with large string sections.

Suggested Records

Numerous rereleases of the swing bands and the songs of the early twentieth century are available. The nearer you can come to re-pressings of original recordings, the better, of course.

Folkways Records has a twelve-record series entitled *Jazz*, which contains many rare re-pressings of interest to historians of the period. The Smithsonian Institution has also rereleased a number of historical recordings, including the *Ziegfeld Follies of 1919* and Cole Porter's show *Anything Goes*, in the 1934 production. The Smithsonian collection *Classic Jazz* has a few useful selections for the study of popular music.

LISTENING GUIDE 1:   "Moonlight Serenade," by the Glenn Miller Orchestra (1939).

This song, the theme song of the supergroup Glenn Miller Orchestra, typifies the ballad of the swing era, a song designed for slow couple dancing. "Moonlight Serenade" was unusual in that it was best known as an instrumental number; most ballads had romantic lyrics.

<u>Melody:</u>   The tune's main characteristic is a long note with an upward-curling triplet at the end. Most of the notes are taken from the diatonic scale, though a number of chromatic notes are found in places. The bridge of the tune shows more variety, moving from major to minor, then back to the original key.

<u>Harmony:</u>   Most of the chords are the tightly placed, dense harmonizations typical of swing. The harmonies are not very adventurous; chords generally resolve in the expected ways, and the piece never varies far from the original key. Chord color—the specific quality of the harmony—is very important to the overall effect of the piece.

<u>Rhythm:</u>   The underlying beat is the slow plunk, plunk marked by the string bass. Nothing fancy here; this is a song for dancing slowly, dreaming, holding your partner close. . . . On another level, however, there is a subtle interplay between the melody rhythm and the accompanying figure played by muted trumpets:

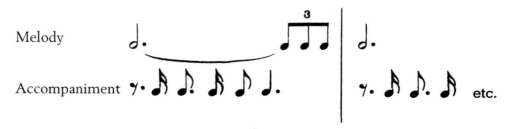

The accompanying part fills in the long melody note with some sort of motion, keeping the effect from being too static.

Instruments: The Miller Orchestra typified the classic swing band, with its three (or four) trumpets, an equal number of trombones, five saxes (two altos, two tenors, a baritone), and the usual rhythm section (piano, guitar, bass, and drums). Because it evolved from the Dixieland band, with its horn line and rhythm section, the swing band originally had no strings except guitar and bass.

Form: The overall form of the song is the venerable AABA structure. The A section, however, is unusual in that it is twelve measures long, rather than the customary eight or sixteen measures. Twelve measures is, of course, the length of a blues period, and although this song is by no means a blues, it does also have an a a^1 b melodic structure within the A phrase. The B section, or bridge, is a conventional eight-bar phrase. The original recording of the song has time for two full statements of the entire melody, plus a coda, and lasts about two and a half minutes. Swing tunes were all about that length, since they had to fit on one side of a ten-inch 78-rpm disc.

Special Effects: Swing-band brass sections made extensive use of a variety of mutes—straight, cup, Solotone, Harmon, and wa-wa, among others. In the beginning of this piece, the trumpets are muted; later they play without mutes. The use of mutes greatly enlarged the number of color effects possible for the arrangers.

LISTENING GUIDE 2: "Doggin' Around," by Count Basie and His Orchestra (1938). (Note: "Doggin' Around" is included in the Smithsonian collection of *Classic Jazz*.)

The other basic type of popular song (besides a ballad) was the dance-oriented, up-tempo *jump* tune. Songs like this one gave the exhibitionists a chance to show off their athletic jitterbugging skill on the dance floor.

Melody: Obviously the melody is not very important here. What melody there is consists of short, fragmented phrases of no great intrinsic interest. The bridge consists simply of a progression of chords.

Harmony: Where the Glenn Miller piece used four- and five-note chords, this piece settles for three- and sometimes four-note chords. The harmonic progression is basic and straightforward, with no surprises. Chord color is used less for mood, and more simply to indicate the flow of the piece.

Rhythm: Rhythm is all, or nearly all, in a fast dance tune. The basic beat is quick, but rock-steady, and reinforced by both bass and drums, four notes to the bar. Various syncopated riffs sparkle against this steady beat, creating an irresistible dance impulse. There are few subtleties here; the rhythm drives, insists, compels.

Instruments: Fewer notes in the chords, fewer instruments in the band. Basie's group here has three trumpets, three trombones, four saxes (two alto, two tenor), piano, bass, drums, and sometimes guitar. Such a group was balanced, flexible, dynamic, and economical.

Form: The basic structure is again AABA, with eight-measure phrases throughout. Variety is obtained by having various members of the band ad-lib solos while other instruments riff in the background to provide interesting accompaniments.

Special Effects: In the opening saxophone chorus the trumpets do a bit of light-hearted growling. In the following saxophone chorus, the trumpets riff a background; then, when the trumpet player solos, the saxes riff. Near the end, the drummer takes a relatively long break, and the entire ensemble plays a brief close.

3 BLACKS AND BLUES

Black people have been part of American life since Spanish America imported African slaves early in the 1500s. The English colonies became parties to commerce in human lives when a shipment of African slaves arrived in Jamestown, Virginia, in 1619.

Slaves were imported to serve as laborers. It would never have occurred to the slave traders to advertise the cultural qualities of their "merchandise." Yet the Africans who came here in chains, and their descendants, kept alive elements of their vital native culture, including music. In time, those elements transformed the music of their white masters and created a new American musical language.

Characteristics of Black American Music

The black American music that evolved on this continent through the end of the Civil War has certain typical qualities. It is virtually all *folk music*, songs and pieces by anonymous composers who passed it on by example to other performers. Few blacks had the training to write the music down, and few whites thought the songs worthy of being notated.

These songs fall into three broad categories—*work songs, religious songs*, and *entertainment songs*. In practice, of course, these categories overlap a great deal. Work songs often have religious references in their texts, and spirituals can be sung just for entertainment.

"Field hollers" and other agricultural labor songs are work songs that were used mainly to express the singer's feelings ("Oh, boys, I'm gwine 'way from heah!") or just pass the time. Other work songs, such as "Long John" or "Take This Hammer," are work-coordinating songs, setting a beat and a timing for several people to perform a task in unison.

Religious songs, such as the well-known *spirituals*, sometimes narrate snatches of biblical stories. They often were given accompaniments by simple instruments such as the tambourine. Some religious songs served as accompaniments for shuffle dances called ring shouts. Freedom songs like "Wade in the Water" often had strong religious associations, as the slaves identified strongly with the ancient Israelites in their struggle for freedom.

Entertainment songs include songs and instrumental pieces designed for amusement or to accompany dancing. Other songs included in this category are lullabies such as "Momma's Gonna Buy Me a Little Lap Dog" and ballads like "John Henry."

Ballads—that is, songs that tell a story over several verses—are not typical black American song forms. Spirituals and work songs seldom narrate a continuous story; rather, each verse is a short sketch of an incident or else a statement of a feeling or reaction. The ballad form is typical of white folk music, and represents white influence on black American music.

Another trait of early black American music is the preference for singing short, repeated phrases. The spiritual "Swing Low, Sweet Chariot" is a model for these short phrases. The longest phrase ("I looked over Jordan and what did I see?") is only nine words long; most phrases are considerably shorter. Both music and words have a great amount of repetition.

SWING LOW, SWEET CHARIOT

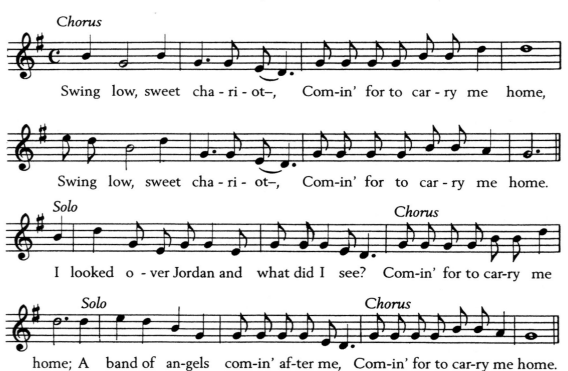

Still another characteristic of black American music can be seen in the song above. Notice that some parts of the song are marked "Solo," and are to be sung by one singer. Other parts, marked "Chorus," are sung by several persons, answering the solo part. This technique, known as *call-and-response singing*, can also be found in African music.

If you heard a performance of this spiritual by a black gospel choir, you might notice that the chorus sings their part the same each time, but the soloist sings somewhat differently each time. Here are two possible versions of the first line:

This technique of *melodic variation by improvisation* is another characteristic of black American music.

In the folk tradition, the singers—most notably the soloists—use a rich vocal quality with a quick, wide vibrato and a great amount of vocal color, ranging from hoarse to mellow to gravelly to shouty. The music has a marked, steady pulse, or basic beat, and the song is performed with great rhythmic intensity, including strong syncopations.

All of these characteristics—short, repeated phrases, call-and-response performance, improvised melodic variation, vocal quality, quick vibrato, rhythmic intensity—come from African musical traditions that survived the rigors of slavery in the New World. So strong are these qualities in black music that they can be heard clearly in popular black performers today, groups like the Temptations or singers like Tina Turner. We shall also see that they can be heard in lots of white music.

The Birth of the Blues

No one knows when the *blues* was born. * No one person can rightly claim the invention of this most durable and versatile of American musical structures. Blues is folk music, and it existed as folk music for some time before it got written down. The

---

* That's right, "was." "Blues" is singular, as in "a blues."

best we can say is that at some time, probably after the Civil War, black folk musicians began "singing the blues."

When we say, "I've got the blues," we mean, "I feel low; I'm unhappy; things aren't going well for me." It seems reasonable, then, that a blues would be sad, mournful music. Many blues songs are indeed sad, but sadness is not what makes a blues a blues. Not all sad songs are blues; not all blues are sad songs. Confused? Let's sort it out a bit.

Technically, a blues must have certain specific qualities. First of all, a classic (that is, in its essential form) blues has a musical period that is twelve measures (or bars) long. This twelve-bar period is subdivided into three phrases, each four bars in length. Each phrase, in turn, comprises a sung portion and an instrumental response called a break. In diagram, the whole musical period looks like this:

Period (12 bars)

phrase 1 (4 bars) phrase 2 (4 bars) phrase 3 (4 bars)

2 2 2 2 2 2

singing break singing break singing break

The sung portion, or text, consists of two phrases, a statement and a response. The statement is repeated to complete the three musical phrases:

phrase A: A pop song can have any form you choose,

phrase A: Oh, yes, a pop song can have any form you choose,

phrase B: But you must have three phrases in a blues!

The text phrase covers two bars of the musical phrase, and the instrument fills in the other two bars with the break. Notice that the formal pattern of the text is AAB.

There are also certain harmonic conventions in a classic blues. Certain chords, or their standard substitutes, should appear in certain measures. In the key of C, the following chords make up a *blues progression*:

MEASURE	1*	2	3	4	5*	6	7*	8	9*	10	11*	12
CHORD	C	C	C	C	F	F	C	C	G	G/F	C	C
CHORD NUMBER	I	I	I	I	IV	IV	I	I	V	V/IV	I	I

The asterisks (*) mark the most important chords in progression. These chords, or their substitutes, must appear in these measures or the piece won't sound like a blues. Other chords may be substituted more freely in other measures. The chord in measure 10 is usually either a V or a IV chord, which are used about equally, so they are both presented as possibilities. Try them both in the progression to see which you prefer.

A blues song usually uses a special scale called (reasonably enough) a blues scale for the melody. The blues scale is like a minor scale, except that certain alternative notes may be chosen:

This is how a melody written in the blues scale might look:

Play this blues phrase with the chords several times. Notice how all the alternative notes of the blues scale are used. Notice also that the "blue notes" (the minor-scale ones) sometimes clash with the basic chord. This is typical, and is part of what makes a blues sound like a blues. Notice also that the harmonization follows the rules, but that certain chords are modified in the nonessential measures.

A blues, then, is a song with a twelve-bar period, three four-bar phrases, and an AAB text pattern. It employs a blues scale and specific chords in specific measures and alternates text with instrumental breaks.

The text of a blues can be about any subject, but it most often deals with feeling low—I lost my job, my boyfriend (or girlfriend) left me, I don't like this town, and so on. Good blues lyrics are not self-pitying, however. Rather, they suggest a tough-minded approach to trouble. "I got to get to work now, get another start," says one singer after lamenting a love affair gone wrong. The blues were a way of dealing with disappointment or adversity.

Blues is not a ballad form; each verse is a complete statement that describes one's feelings or circumstances. A blues can be fast or slow, happy or sad, simple or complicated, sung with a guitar, or accompanied by a band roaring all stops out. If it has the qualities described above, it's still a blues—one of the most distinctive song forms in the world, and uniquely American.

Gospel Music

Blues is a secular song form; there could be religious blues, I suppose, but I've never heard one. Besides the spiritual, which was closely associated with slavery, the most important black sacred-music style is the *gospel* song. There is no particular formal structure for the gospel song, as there is for a blues. When a gospel song is performed with choir accompaniment, there is often quite a bit of call-and-response singing. As with other types of black music, the choir's part is often a short response sung exactly the same each time, while the soloist's part is much more free and improvised.

Like blues and jazz, gospel music is usually highly rhythmic and syncopated. It often uses instrumental accompaniment—piano, organ, rhythm instruments, even horns and guitars. People raised on the staid, foursquare traditions of white hymns feel vaguely uneasy about church music being rhythmic and jazzy. They often feel that the lively beat trivializes the religious feeling of the music. For gospel singers and their audiences, however, the rhythm helps generate the desired religious enthusiasm.

Black musicians have found it easy to change from sacred to secular music. Several popular performers and groups—among them Ray Charles, Aretha Franklin, and Tina Turner—began as church gospel music singers. The harmonies and the rhythm that they learned in church translate readily into the idiom of popular music.

Country Blues and City Rhythm-and-Blues

Blues developed in the hands and songs of self-taught country musicians who most often accompanied themselves on a guitar. Sometimes these folk performers used a piece of steel, a jackknife, or the neck broken off a bottle to intensify the tone of the melody part of the guitar accompaniment. This practice explains the term "bottleneck guitar" to describe this type of playing.

Country blues drifted into the city and quickly became more sophisticated. The accompanying instrument often became a piano instead of a guitar. Other instruments—such as the cornet, the clarinet, and the trombone—soon joined the piano and gave rise to jazz. Later, especially during the 1930s and 1940s, a city type of blues, with drums, horns, and other instruments, evolved. This faster and less soulful (but more popular) style was called *rhythm-and-blues*, or *R & B*.

Rhythm-and-blues borrowed the basic blues structure and scale from classic country blues and gave it upbeat treatment and often frivolous texts. Titles like "Easy Rider Blues" or "Perdido Street Blues" were replaced by names like "Good Golly Miss Molly" or "Caldonia." The country singers' need for expression gave way to the city kids' craving for rhythm, motion, and dancing. Performed by a host of black musicians, R & B became the most popular music of large segments of America's black population for many years. It remained an ethnic music, listened and danced to by black audiences, until the early 1950s. Then, the music of men like Chuck Berry, Little Richard, Fats Domino, and Chubby Checker exploded on the world under the name of *rock 'n' roll.*

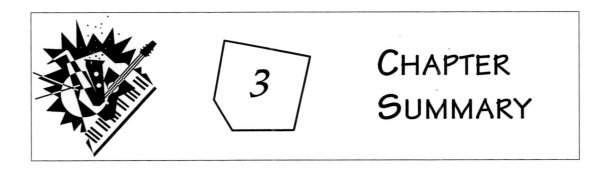

3   CHAPTER SUMMARY

Many musical traits entered the New World along with African slaves. Chief Among these were call-and-response singing, a distinctive vocal style, a dynamic rhythmic sense, a fondness for improvisation, and a love of instruments. Black musicians created the black spiritual and the blues as their sacred and secular means of musical expression. Both kinds of music live on in new forms, the spiritual as gospel music, and the blues transformed into rhythm-and-blues.

Suggested Projects

1. Lots of songs with "blues" in their titles aren't actually blues song. Try to find music for the following songs and discover which ones are really blues: "Birth of the Blues"; "St. Louis Blues"; "Blues in the Night"; "I've Got a Right to Sing the Blues"; "Blue Suede Shoes."

2. Listen to examples of gospel music; write down the characteristics of what you hear. Now listen to some early rock 'n' roll, and note its musical characteristics. Compare lists to see which characteristics are common, and which are distinctive.

3. Research the following question: What was happening in the United States between 1910 and 1950 that might have caused country blues to give way to rhythm-and-blues?

Suggested Records

Berry, Chuck. *Rockit*. Atco 38-118.

Domino, Fats. *Million Sellers*. United Artists LM 1027.

Jackson, Mahalia. *I Sing Because I'm Happy*. Folkways 31101.

Jazz, Vol. II: The Blues. Folkways FJ 2802.

Music Down Home. Folkways FA 2691.

Roots: The Rock and Roll Sound of Louisiana and Mississippi. Folkways FJ 2865.

Suggested Books

Shaw, Arnold. *The World of Soul*. New York: Cowles Book Company, 1970.

Oliver, Paul. *The Story of the Blues*. Philadelphia: Chilton Book Company, 1969.

Redd, Lawrence. *Rock Is Rhythm and Blues*. Lansing, MI: Michigan State University Press, 1974.

Southern, Eileen. *The Music of Black Americans*. New York: W.W. Norton and Company, Inc., 1971.

4 WHERE THE BLUEGRASS GROWS

Think for a moment about the family names of the students in your class. Smith and Jones; Carter and Fletcher; Hoffman and Schultz; LeClerc and Hebert; Goldstein and Strauss; Sczepanski and Mazanowski; Chervenko and Nemenoff; Caluzzi and Barbaro; Sanchez and Romero; and, increasingly, Cheung, Ngo, Tamura, Rao, and Tsai. What's the message? Ours is indeed a nation of immigrants, a nation of minorities, a people fashioned out of all the peoples of the earth.

It was so from the beginnings of our nation. Spanish settlers staked out portions of Florida in the 1500s. Spanish governors and friars brought the (sometimes dubious) advantages of "civilization" to the Pueblo Indians of the Southwest—people who were already quite civilized. French adventurers explored the Mississippi and Ohio River valleys, giving names to places like Detroit, Des Moines, Marquette, and Duquesne. Dutch settlers moved into the Hudson Valley and built Harlem and Schuylkill and Schenectady. German immigrants named Hanover in Pennsylvania, Rhinelander in Wisconsin, and Frankenmuth in Michigan. New York, New London, Winchester, and Salem all reveal America's debt to the English; Indian names—Menominee, Wisconsin; Erie, Pennsylvania; Wyandotte, Michigan; Shenandoah, Virginia; Dahlonega, Georgia; Yakima, Washington; Moenkopi, Arizona—freckle every state's map.

We're used to this now, and we take it for granted. We can drive from Pontiac, Michigan, through Detroit; past Windsor, Ontario; to Dearborn and Ypsilanti; then through Albion and Portage; over to Kalamazoo; then turn north through Otsego to Wyoming; end up in Holland—and think of all of these as good American place names. Indeed they are now, but they once represented peoples who were very different from one another. These peoples had their own cultures, languages, customs, and their own music. American folk music, therefore, is like a river that receives water from all of these little streams, and many more.

Characteristics of White American Folk Music

The largest of the early streams came from the British Isles and from western and central Europe. English, Irish, and Scottish settlers predominated in the thirteen original American colonies, with smatterings of Germans, French, and Dutch. Since the folk music of these cultures is much alike, this musical style became the basic one in America. Let's examine the main characteristics of that style.

The main song form of the white settlers was the ballad, a song that relates a story over several verses. Ballads deal with common and familiar themes: love and hate (often in the same song); victory over enemies; famous disasters; important people. Death is a common theme in these Anglo-American ballads. In "Barbara Allen," for example, a young man dies of unrequited love for her. She spurned him in life, but then feels guilty about his death, and so dies herself. In "The Death of Queen Jane," a queen of England dies in childbirth but produces an heir for the king. Another ballad tells of a jealous girl who drowns her pretty sister in order to have the sister's boyfriend. The sister returns as a ghost and kills her killer. Not all ballads are so morbid, but the gruesome ones were quite popular—three centuries before horror movies.

The stories were the most important features of ballads, and were sung to standard melodies, sometimes two or three melodies serving one story. Singers might change the song slightly, but they tried to sing it as nearly as possible to the way they learned it. In other words, there was little or no improvisation in ballad singing. Singers also told the story with as little personal involvement as possible. They tried to be as anonymous as a newscaster—which, in the centuries before radio and TV, is exactly what they were. They would sing about "the blood and the gore/which spilled on the floor" with the same detachment with which they would announce, "the cantaloupes are ripe."

Anglo-American ballads are solo songs, with one person narrating the story. They were originally sung without any instrumental accompaniment, but on this side of the Atlantic, they were often enhanced by a guitar, banjo, or dulcimer. The singer's vocal quality was soloistic, too, nasal and harsh and tense, rather than mellow and blending.

Not all songs were ballads, of course. There were work songs and nonsense songs, seasonal songs, lullabies, and entertainment songs, among others. Dance tunes, whether sung or played, were also quite popular. These were often based on traditional Irish or Scottish jigs and dance melodies, and were usually played on a fiddle.

In the cities of the Colonies and the early Republic, the musical fashions of Europe were closely followed and imitated. In rural areas, however, the old songs were still sung in the old ways, and city folk looked on their country cousins as uncultured hicks. Those rural areas where little influence from outside was felt grew more and more apart from the well-traveled areas in their culture and their music. These people, who often lived in valleys in the Appalachian Mountains, were nicknamed hillbillies.

By the beginning of this century, vocal and instrumental folk music had become common throughout the rural sections of the South and the Midwest. When southern workers moved north to work in factories during World War I, they brought the old songs and styles with them. In the same fashion, midwestern farmers driven from their land by the Dust Bowl years of the 1930s made a ready market for down-home music in California, where they resettled.

The market was there, indeed, but until the 1920s, satisfying it depended on being able to attend a live performance. Radio and the recording industry concentrated on popular stars, and considered hillbilly music unworthy of production. However, certain stations in the South began broadcasting folk, or hillbilly, performances as early as 1922. Station WBAP in Fort Worth, Texas, began putting them on the air periodically, and by 1927, gave country music a regular Friday night program.

Early Recordings

The year 1922 also marked the first recording of a country-music record. Country fiddlers Eck Robertson, dressed in a Confederate soldier's uniform, and Henry Gilliland, decked out in a cowboy outfit, marched into the RCA Victor studios in New York and demanded an audition. It is not recorded what the good folks at RCA thought of this duo, but they did record them, and hillbilly music was immortalized in wax (or, more accurately, in shellac). After a fitful beginning, the ballads and breakdowns acquired an audience of millions of eager listeners and buyers. Recording companies combed the South, setting up studios in barns and warehouses to record everyone who could strum a "git-tar" and wail a mournful song. Like early jazz recordings, the results of this endeavor were uneven in quality. Nonetheless, many priceless recordings of authentic folk styles were made through these early commercial efforts.

The record companies that made these early country-music recordings (labeled "hillbilly" in their catalogues) were the same ones that recorded early jazz (labeled "race" records in their catalogues)—Okeh, Vocalion, Brunswick, Gennett, along with Columbia and RCA Victor. Sears Roebuck and Montgomery Ward sold hillbilly records through their mail-order departments. Since country performers usually got a flat fee—$25 or so with no royalties—for each recording, the record companies could afford to record many performers. The hit performances paid for a lot of poor or mediocre recordings.

Early Performers and Songs

The names of early country-music performers are largely Anglo-Saxon in origin—names like Uncle Dave Macon, Riley Puckett, Buell Kazee and Bradley Kincaid, Gideon Tanner and Pop Stoneman, and Maybelle Carter. Some were singers, and many were prominent instrumentalists who played fiddle, banjo or guitar. Names of groups from those early years might be sentimental or wryly comical. Names such as the Carter Family or the North Carolina Ramblers vied with the Original Hillbillies, the Dixie Mountaineers, and Gid Tanner and His Skillet Lickers.

The repertoire of these country performers borrowed heavily from traditional Anglo-American ballads, with songs like "The Wreck on the Southern Old 97," "Little Rosewood Casket," "The Titanic," and the durable "Barbara Allen." Instruments included the banjo, guitar, and fiddle; sometimes a piano or mandolin might be added. Occasionally, popular tunes from Tin Pan Alley worked their way into the repertoire. Some country performers, like Dock Boggs, occasionally recorded a blues learned from black rural musicians. Some, like Buell Kazee and Vernon Dalhart (real name: Marion Slaughter), had classical training as singers. Most of them were not professional musicians, but worked in mills or as farmers, and moonlighted as country musicians.

As the 1920s passed, two general styles emerged in hillbilly music—country music and mountain or bluegrass music. *Mountain music* comprised the older songs and ballads of the Appalachians, performed in the traditional ways. *Country music,* on the other hand, borrowed more in style and repertoire from current popular music. At this period, the western image that is so important today was not a part of the country scene. That change was made in the 1930s, and one of the central influences was the man known as *the Blue Yodeler*—Jimmie Rodgers.

Jimmie Rodgers

The first country singer of star caliber was a tall, slender man with a wide and friendly grin. He was born James Charles Rodgers, in Mississippi in 1897. His father was a railroad gang foreman; his mother died when he was only four. The family knocked around the rural South following the father's job, which took them from one stretch of broken track to another. This traveling life brought young Jimmie into contact with many different cultures—black and white, Cajun French and Creole Spanish—that filled the region.

Beginning as a water boy, Jimmie worked for the railroads for fourteen years. He worked his way up to flagman and brakeman, but developed tuberculosis, which forced him to give up the vigorous outdoor life. At age twenty-eight, Jimmie was in forced retirement, looking for another way to make a living. He had learned to play guitar and banjo as a boy, so he joined a minstrel troupe that traveled from town to town. He and his wife Carrie settled in Asheville, North Carolina, hoping the mountain climate would ease the distress of his illness. Here he was discovered by an agent for RCA Victor. By the end of 1927, Victor found that it had a budding star in its stable.

His most famous trademark was the "blue yodel," a yodeling section tacked onto an approximation of the Negro blues form. Performing on radio and recording, in tent shows and theaters throughout the South, Rodgers soon became the most popular singer in country music. When his disease forced him to move to the drier Texas climate, he focused his touring on the southwestern states. Despite the efforts to overcome his illness, he succumbed in 1933, at age thirty-six. Jimmie Rodgers left behind a legacy that has affected every country singer since.

Early Country Radio Shows

Exactly which radio station first broadcast a country singer or instrumentalist will probably never be known for sure. We can be sure, however, that Atlanta's station WSB was one of the very earliest, for it featured hillbilly music as early as 1922. Another early leader in this field was WBAP in Fort Worth, Texas, which inaugurated the "radio barn dance." Chicago's station WLS began a popular series called National Barn Dance that was broadcast weekly beginning in 1924. A year later, Nashville's station WSM launched a Saturday night program originally called Barn Dance. The name was later changed to Grand Ole Opry, and it's still going strong.

The early hillbilly programs featured mainly instrumental music, often fiddle soloists like M.J. Bonner and eighty-year-old Uncle Jimmy Thompson. Sometimes string bands appeared, with names like the Gully Jumpers or the Fruit Jar Drinkers. Vocalists, especially pop-influenced ballad crooners, were a later addition to country music. Among the earliest of these country singers to achieve real importance were Uncle Dave Macon and Jimmie Rodgers.

Gene Autry and the Cowboy Image

Country and western is the common classification for the type of music heard on Grand Ole Opry. You have probably noticed that, so far, we've talked a lot about "country" and not much about "western." This is because, until the 1930s, country music was southern, hillbilly music, with none of the cowboy trimmings that are now so essential. One of the most influential people in making that change was a Texas-born, guitar-strumming Oklahoma telegraph operator named Gene Autry.

Far from being a Texas cowboy, Autry was born on a tenant farm in East Texas—land that had more in common with Arkansas and Louisiana than with the rangelands. Autry's musical idol was Jimmie Rodgers. When he wasn't busy at the telegraph key, he strummed his guitar and sang good imitations of his hero, tunes he had learned from recordings. Fate, in the person of famous cowboy humorist Will Rogers (no kin to Jimmie), stopped by the little Oklahoma station where Gene worked. Rogers listened to Autry sing, and urged him to go to New York to make records. Gene was as self-confident as the next man, but giving up a secure job to dash off to New York with no contract looked awfully like a wild-goose chase. So he stayed where he was for the time being, but fate wouldn't take no for an answer. Within a few years, Gene lost his job with the railroad, a victim of the 1929 depression. Before the year was out, Victor Records was offering songs sung by Gene Autry, the Oklahoma Cowboy.

Success in recordings soon earned Autry a regular spot on the WLS Barn Dance program in Chicago. As his popularity grew, he recorded on the Sears Roebuck label, and Gene Autry songbooks and guitar instruction manuals appeared. Autry had never punched a cow or roped a steer, but he became the very image of the singing cowboy in the minds of millions of easterners. His Hollywood career, beginning in 1934 and spanning more than one hundred cinema productions, solidified that image for all time. Hillbilly music, slicked up and buttoned down with pearl studs, suddenly had a national audience. Masquerading as cowboy tunes, country and western had arrived.

The legion of other country performers with a western image includes many strong personalities—Texans like Ernest Tubb and Tex Ritter, talented songwriter Bob Nolan (a Canadian by birth), and well-known Ohioan Leonard Slye, also known as Roy Rogers.

The typical western ensemble of the period included the classic hillbilly fiddle-and-guitar combination, but added a string bass and often a Hawaiian steel guitar, electrically amplified. Arrangements became steadily more mellow and slick as the 1930s gave way to the war years of the early 1940s. Vocal groups like the Sons of the Pioneers produced smooth, blended harmonies modeled on swing vocal groups like the Modernaires or the Andrews Sisters.

Country Music During World War II

All wars disrupt the societies they afflict. Modern wars create social turmoil not only in the lands where they are fought, but also in rear areas and even in neutral nations. World War II was the most disruptive war in world history.

The war caused the migration of hundreds of thousands of southern rural folk to the northern cities to work in war plants. The black folk who migrated brought the blues to the city, where it became rhythm-and-blues. The white folk brought hillbilly music to the city, where it, too, picked up urban sophistications to appeal to a new, wider market.

Even before the United States entered the war, country music received an unexpected assist from the recording industry. Composers of concert music, Broadway shows, popular songs, and other types of music usually belonged to the American Society of Composers, Authors, and Publishers (ASCAP for short). This organization represented its members, helped collect royalties, and protected their legal rights. Not everyone could join ASCAP; one had to be approved by its Membership Committee. The Committee did not recognize the craft of hillbilly composers as "real" music, and few country-music writers were represented.

At the beginning of 1941, ASCAP got into a confrontation with the radio networks over licensing fees for its members' music, and the organization refused to give the networks permission to perform any ASCAP-protected music. The networks retaliated by forming their own protective group for composers, called Broadcast Music, Inc. (BMI). This group operated in the same way as ASCAP, but it needed to find composers who weren't already members of the rival organization. It discovered a vast market in the country-and-western and rhythm-and-blues musicians. Radio stations began playing country music in parts of the nation that had never heard it before. When ASCAP and the networks settled their dispute ten months later, BMI—and country music—were firmly established nationwide.

When the country people moved north to the factories, or entered the military services, there was a country-music establishment ready to entertain them with the sounds and songs of home. This was the era of Roy Acuff and Ernest Tubb, of Tex Ritter and Jimmie Davis, of Eddie Arnold and Red Foley. By now (thanks partly to Gene Autry and Roy Rogers), the western garb was standard for all country groups. The instruments were fixed into a basic fiddle-guitar-string-bass ensemble, with banjo or steel guitar common, and with more and more electric amplification.

The Postwar Years: 1945–1954

The end of World War II brought a boom in popular music of all sorts. Returning GI's had cash and were hungry for the taste, touch, and sound of home. Through the BMI experience, and because of the increasing business expertise of country musicians, hillbilly composers and performers were finally in a position to make a living from their music.

A sign of their newly-won respect was the change in listing of country music in *Billboard* magazine, the record trade's most important journal. From mid-1949 on, *Billboard* dropped the "hillbilly" record category and listed records as "country and western." Another sign was the number of country songs that were performed by pop singers like Bing Crosby. A third sign was the number of country singers who could afford to own Cadillacs. At any rate, the country song and style and the amplified guitar ensemble had secured a permanent place on the American musical scene. The time was now ripe for a merger of dressed-up white rural southern music with dressed-up black rural southern music to form a new popular-music style. That style would be called rock 'n' roll.

CHAPTER SUMMARY

4

White American music is based primarily on the English and West European folk style, with its ballads sung in narrative fashion and its fondness for dance music played by small bands of instruments. By the beginning of this century, the old songs were considered "hick," and were referred to as hillbilly music. Nonetheless, tens of thousands of loyal fans made a ready market for recordings and radio, and made possible the gradual transition to the country-and-western genre. Singers like Jimmie Rodgers, Gene Autry, Roy Rogers, and Ernest Tubb expanded the repertoire and added new sophistications to "C & W." By World War II, the standard C & W band had emerged, with guitars, string bass, Hawaiian guitar, and occasionally drums. One could hear country music on city radio stations and jukeboxes. Both the musicians and the studio production had grown much more skillful and slick. Hick music had grown up.

Suggested Projects

1. Many of the songs performed by early country musicians were versions of English ballads such as the Child ballads. Do a research report on English balladry, especially the Child ballads and "broadside" ballads.

2. Listen to programs of the Grand Ole Opry. What differences in the songs do you notice as compared with pop or rock music? What similarities are there?

3. It might be instructive to make a display of country singers, noting how many stress the cowboy/cowgirl image. Compare this image to the texts of the songs, noticing how many have a western theme. Don't overlook such performers as Charlie Daniels, Boxcar Willie, and Slim Whitman.

Suggested Books

Malone, Bill. *Country Music, USA.* Austin, TX: University of Texas Press, 1968. This excellent and scholarly work is written in an easy-reading style, and will likely be the definitive book on the subject for some time.

Suggested Records

Acuff, Roy. *Roy Acuff Sings Hank Williams.* Elektra 287.

Arnold, Eddy. *Best of Eddy Arnold.* RCA AYL1-3675.

Atkins, Chet. *Best of Chet On the Road.* RCA AHL1-3515.

Bluegrass Banjo. Archive of Folk and Jazz Music 357.

Flatt, Lester. *Fantastic Pickin'.* CMH 6232.

The Smithsonian Institution has recently released a record set of country music. It includes many of the very early groups, Jimmie Rodgers, Uncle Dave Macon, and others. For information, write Smithsonian Institution, P.O. Box 2456, Washington, DC 20013.

5 THE BEGINNINGS OF ROCK AND ROLL

The deluge began in 1953. That was the year that a boisterous group called Bill Haley and the Comets (a pun on Halley's Comet; never mind that the spelling isn't the same) released a jangling single called "Crazy Man Crazy." The song welded country-and-western singers and instruments to the infectious rhythm-and-blues beat, and set millions of adolescent bodies into gyrating motion. Rock 'n' roll had hit the beach, and soon captured everything in sight.

To their older brothers and sisters, raised on the lilting sophistication of big-band swing, the young rock 'n' rollers' musical tastes seemed vulgar and primitive. To their parents, never entirely reconciled to jitterbugging and swooning over Frank Sinatra, rock 'n' roll seemed barbarous, a musical concoction crafted by the dregs of society. Few of them recalled that *their* parents had expressed the same objections to the jazz songs, the animal dances, the "Oh, you kid" moral laxity of their own teen years.[*]

More than a generation gap yawned between the supporters of Artie Shaw and Tommy Dorsey and the wriggling, jiggling Presley partisans. The new music was more than just *new*, it was *revolutionary*. It rejected the sound, the rhythm, the instruments, the singing style, the very aesthetic of swing. It was no outgrowth of previous trends; it was, instead, a radical departure from them. One took sides: one liked swing, and loathed rock 'n' roll; or one identified totally with the rockers, and had no truck with the old stuff. There was very little middle ground.

Reasons for Rock 'n' Roll's Popularity

It is not enough to note the details of what happened; one has to delve further to understand *why* this revolution in taste occurred. There is no one final reason, of

---

[*] The expression comes from a line in a song: "I love my wife, but oh, you kid!"

course, for human history is seldom that simple. However, some important factors in the process can be described.

One important factor was that swing, as a popular, expressive idiom, had blown itself out. Like biological organisms, musical styles go through phases of birth, growth, maturity, and decay. Musicians strive to stay always fresh and innovative. The early big bands had evolved over a decade into the lean, tight, rhythmic groups of classic swing in the period 1936–42. The instrumentation was relatively fixed at three to four trumpets, three to four trombones, five saxes, and four rhythm pieces. This was the band size of Goodman, Dorsey, Glenn Miller, Count Basie, Duke Ellington—and probably of a few hundred other band leaders of varying degrees of fame.

After World War II, swing was searching for a new sound. The old band sound had become trite. Instruments were added—four or five trumpets or trombones, six saxophones, extra people in the rhythm section. Some bands added full string sections to the winds and percussion, making great, lush, unwieldy groups that usually lacked rhythmic punch. As even these experiments grew tiresome, some groups experimented with novel instrumentations with some short-term success. One group, for example, featured a vocalist, French horns, and a rhythm section. It was obvious that swing, as an expressive idiom, was in serious difficulty.

A second factor was the economic circumstances of rock's rise. The classic swing bands had kept a good size for touring, as well as making recordings and playing on radio. Much of the groups' appeal was generated at proms and dances, where young listeners could experience the music live and identify with the performers' personalities. The classic band of fifteen to sixteen performers was big enough to be distinctive but small enough to travel well. The small symphonies that emerged after the war were suited to recording and radio performances, but were too cumbersome and expensive to travel well. The much smaller (and increasingly electrically amplified) rock 'n' roll bands had an enormous economic advantage, and could achieve the personal touch now denied the older groups.

Still another reason for the change could be found in the young rock 'n' rollers themselves. Rock 'n' roll's greatest appeal was to the youngsters who had been born during or just before World War II. It is difficult today to realize the emotional stresses that afflicted people then—the unrelieved tension of the war, with its shortages and rationing, its headlines of disaster and triumph, and the constant nagging worry about the well-being of family members in the service. The end of the war brought joy and relief—but also the horrors of the extermination camps and the awesome image of a mushroom-shaped cloud. The old foes, Japan and Germany, were soon replaced by a new opponent, the Soviet Union. The newsreels were filled with stories of spy trials, nuclear bomb tests, and aircraft flying into Berlin to keep the city alive. In 1950, the Korean War started, and we were in a shooting war again. The times were tense, and the tension wore heavily on youngsters who could scarcely understand the world in which they lived.

Rock 'n' roll offered diversion and relief from this world. First and foremost, it was body music, appealing directly to the dancing impulse. The relentless beat, the simple harmonies, the rudimentary and often ungrammatical texts ("You Ain't Nothin' But a Hound Dog"), and the brash, irreverent high spirits of the music celebrated youth and good times. It helped block out the somber import of the news.

Characteristics of Rock 'n' Roll

Rock 'n' roll borrowed from bluegrass music, and even more heavily from rhythm-and-blues. The former contributed the guitar-based ensemble, the country accents of many of the singers, and the story lines of some of the songs. Black rhythm-and-blues provided the great majority of rock 'n' roll's characteristics. To begin with, many rock 'n' roll songs, including "Hound Dog" and "Rock Around the Clock," use the durable blues form—twelve-measure phrases, specific chords in specific measures, blue notes, and so on. Certain instruments, especially drums and saxophone, were borrowed from R & B. The way the saxophone was played (growly tone, riffing on one note) also came from black musical style.

The most important characteristic that rock 'n' roll borrowed from rhythm-and-blues, however, is the rhythm itself. The beat, the basic pulse, dominates everything else in the song. Rhythm was ruthlessly stripped of all subtlety. Three main rhythm patterns predominated, and may be found in song after song: 1. Even, duple eighth-note patterns with accents on the second and fourth beats

played absolutely evenly. The accented beats might be emphasized with a tambourine. 2. Lilting triplets in slow tempo, usually accompanied by a stock bass figure that changed pitches to fit the chord changes

but remained fixed in rhythm. 3. A rapid quarter-eighth pattern that produced a loping boogie rhythm.

Rock 'n' roll also contains differences in text from previous popular songs. It is perhaps the first popular music to direct itself specifically at young adolescents. As with all popular music (of this century, at least), love (or its symptoms) is the most popular topic—specifically high-school-age love, as celebrated in such songs as "Puppy Love" or "This Time We're Breaking Up For Good." Other texts, however, deal with the trials of teens in relating to their parents, as in the witty "Yackety Yak," by the Coasters. "Take out the trash, walk the dog, clean your room," say the words, and each chorus ends with, "Yackety yak, don't talk back!" The theme of feeling misunderstood and persecuted is also reflected in "Charlie Brown," in which a bass voice periodically asks, "Why is everybody always pickin' on me?"

The texts often approach sex with a candor that adults found discomfiting, to their children's delight. Black music had long accepted veiled references and double-entendres, and few people missed the suggestion in the line, "I found my thrill on Blueberry Hill." Parents who squirmed when their twelve-year-old daughter sang the song should have remembered the Cole Porter hits of an earlier day. "Love For Sale" and the suggestive "Let's Do It (Let's Fall in Love)" once mortified their parents.

The focus of early rock 'n' roll, however, never shifted away from the impelling rhythmic drive. Texts were kept simple, sometimes inane; harmony was reduced to three or four chords, with the most direct and obvious relationships to one another. Certain harmonic conventions did emerge, such as the I–vi progression (Figure IA) or I-$^{\flat}$VII (Figure IB), or the longer progression I–vi–ii–V7 (Figure IC), and of course, the blues changes mentioned earlier. No subtleties intruded, no blurring of the basic key, no ambiguities of tonality were tolerated. The beat was all.

FIGURE I

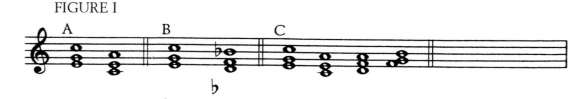

Rock 'n' Roll Singers and Groups

As the stream of rock 'n' roll turned into a flood, and then into a tidal wave, more and more personalities and groups surfaced, most of whom soon sank from sight. Some groups capitalized on a lead singer's name—Ray Peterson, Freddie Cannon (many first names were in diminutive form), Jimmy Gilmer, Buddy Holly, Buddy Knox, Eddie Cochran. First and foremost, though, was Elvis Presley, whose talent and sulky, sexy good looks were hyped into a gigantic commercial phenomenon.

Black performers became major rock 'n' roll personalities as well, even with white audiences—which was something of a novelty in the 1950s. The most influential of these was Chuck Berry, whose songs ("Maybelline," "Roll Over, Beethoven," "Johnny B. Goode") defined the idiom. Fats Domino also achieved a national reputation, as did Bobby Blue Bland, James Brown, Little Richard, Bo Diddley, and many others.

Along with the solo performers or "headliners," some groups also achieved prominence. The groups were sometimes named after animals—the Flamingoes or the Falcons, echoed later by the Beatles and their feeble American copies, the Monkees. Others took names suggesting a mood or feeling, such as the Coasters, the Drifters, the Shadows, or the Impressions. Many of the black rock groups had their origins in church gospel singing groups. Still other groups borrowed someone's name, such as the Everly Brothers or Booker T and the MG's. Aside from the gospel origins, these groups continued a tradition fixed in the swing era by groups such as the Andrews Sisters, the Ink Spots, the Modernaires, and the Lamplighters.

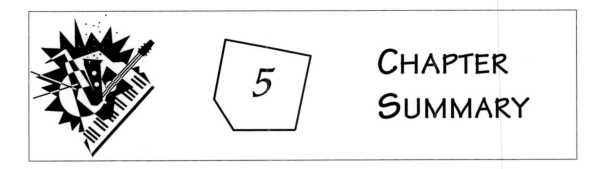

CHAPTER SUMMARY
5

By 1962, rock 'n' roll had established itself as *the* American pop-music idiom. From its first appearance in the early 1950s, this raucous celebration of adolescent high spirits had come to dominate the airwaves both here and abroad. The energetic, blues-based music with its compulsive beat and its cocky lyrics drove more sophisticated, jaded swing into oblivion.

Rock 'n' roll triumphed by being everything that swing was not. Swing was subtle; rock was sledgehammer obvious. Swing used large sections of wind instruments; rock was based on the guitar-bass-drum ensemble. Swing employed sophisticated harmonic effects; rock stuck to folk-tune harmonies. Swing's beat was soft and understated; rock's beat was thunderous. Swing texts were veiled and poetic; rock's verses were crude, sometimes mindless ("doo wopaloo wopalop bop bop"), often juvenile. No one could doubt that a revolution—in sound, in function, in aesthetic—had taken place.

Revolutions have their troubles, though, and these troubles are often the same ones faced by the older regime: How do you keep moving? Once you have done all this, overturned everything, what do you do next? Not surprisingly, revolutions often adopt the same solutions as the institutions they overthrew. It's the same in music; once a new sound is established, it begins to be trite. The old urge to become more subtle and harmonically adventurous, to add new instruments and more interesting arrangements, shows up once again. By 1963, it was apparent that rock 'n' roll had said about all it had to say, and that change was in the wind.

Suggested Projects

1. Listen to Elvis Presley's recording of "Hound Dog," which uses blues changes. Do the changes occur in the expected places? Is the text in typical blues form? Does the song use a twelve-measure phrase? Now listen to Bill Haley's "Rock Around the Clock," and answer the same questions.

2. Find examples of the three rhythm patterns mentioned in this chapter. Are there other typical rock 'n' roll characteristics you can discover? List them.

3. What sort of dances did the young rock 'n' rollers do? See if you can learn to do the twist. Were these dances mostly couple dances or solo dances?

Suggested Records

Berry, Chuck. *Chuck Berry: Golden Decade*. Chess.

Presley, Elvis. *The Elvis Presley Sun Collection*. RCA.

20 Rock Revival Greats. K-Tel NI 4750. A good survey of minor groups and styles of early rock 'n' roll.

6 THE BRITISH ARE COMING!

Liverpool, England is a grimy industrial seaport city on the Mersey River, close to the Irish Sea at the island of Britain's narrow waist. Like seaports everywhere in the world, it caters to a rough, hard-drinking, brawling clientele of sailors from all quarters of the globe. Like industrial cities everywhere, it also provides distractions for mill-hands and machine operators, people whose tastes in entertainment often tend toward the raw, the vital, and the elemental. It's a rough town, Liverpool; a blue-collar town, short on refinements. For entertainers, it's the sort of place where you either please the crowd or they might throw you out—bodily.

In the early 1960s, each dive and cellar club had musical entertainment of some sort—a pianist or a small band—playing for drinks and tips and a small salary from the club's owners. Mostly they played current rock 'n' roll hits from America, tunes by Bill Haley or Buddy Holly or Chuck Berry, interspersed with some of their own material of the same sort. The music had to be simple, and it had to move, if the bands were to keep working. One bad night and they'd be out on their ears. Most performers did something else during the day, but the extra quid earned at night helped pay the bills, so you played what the customers wanted to hear.

One rather typical group in Liverpool in the late 1950s was a four-man band called the Cavemen. They were also known as the Moon-dogs, the Quarrymen Skiffle Group, and the Moonshiners, depending on which club they were working at the time. Three of the Cavemen were rather bored college students by day. They enjoyed playing at night, and would have been happy to make a career of their music. The pay, however, would hardly support an aspiring musician. Fifteen dollars a week wouldn't go far, even in 1960.

When the group got an offer from a club in Hamburg, Germany, for $20 per week, it looked too good to pass up. But what name to use? One of the group thought up a name that was a play on words. In the late 1950s, America's intellectuals went through a period of fascination with the writers who called themselves the Beat Generation. Their deliberately bizarre appearance and behavior earned them the nickname of beatniks. The Cavemen adopted the name the Silver Beatles for their Hamburg job, and it is as the Beatles that they have been known ever since.

The Hamburg job produced nothing much more exciting than a slightly higher salary and one recording. Dame Fate, who chased after Gene Autry until she made him a star, seemed not to notice this unremarkable band of Liverpudlians (isn't that a delicious word?), but the Lady was merely being coy. She located a young department-store heir named Brian Epstein, who in 1961 heard the group's recording and undertook to manage them.

He changed their appearance from grungy beatnik to choirboy cute and arranged for recordings and TV appearances. They replaced their first drummer with Ringo Starr, and the magic circle—John Lennon, Paul McCartney, George Harrison, and Starr—was complete.

This is a good place to think about a question that applies to many entertainers: Why was *this* group to become so popular? There were dozens—perhaps hundreds— of similar bands in Liverpool and all over England, playing similar songs in similar ways. Many of those bands probably had musicians as talented and proficient as any of the Beatles. The quartet themselves had no inflated view of their abilities. Harrison once remarked wistfully that he wished he could be a "really good guitar player," and Lennon once stated that the only thing about their art that they took seriously was the money.

What made the difference in this case was the fifth Beatle, Brian Epstein. However talented a person or a group is, a good promoter can maximize their potential (or minimize their defects). Epstein had a flair for promotion, and by the time he died in 1967, the Beatles could say, in awe but with some justification, "We're more popular than Jesus Christ."

They began by conquering England. In 1963, they earned their first gold record in Britain. Life became a whirl of recording dates, concerts, television appearances, a command performance before the Queen Mother and Princess Margaret. As went England, so went the Continent. "Beatlemania," it was called, and it swept Europe like an epidemic. At almost any time, night or day, if a person turned the radio dial, a Beatle tune was playing on some station.

The United States held out until 1964. At the beginning of January in that year, there were no British groups with songs in *Billboard* magazine's Top 100. Within a month, *Meet the Beatles* was the hottest selling album in the country. The group presented a concert in Carnegie Hall in February, and appeared on Ed Sullivan's televised variety show soon afterward. America surrendered to Beatlemania with mixed delight and apprehension, and shaggy Beatle haircuts appeared from Manhattan to Pacific Palisades.

Parents of teenage daughters who had already been scandalized by Elvis Presley's suggestive wiggling felt distinctly uneasy about "the Moptops" from England. True enough, "I Want to Hold Your Hand" did sound pretty tame. It inspired visions of innocent puppy love, with none of the alarming double meaning of "Sixty Minute Man" or even of "Love Me Tender." But who could make sense of ditties like, "It's Been a Hard Day's Night?" Besides, if these Brits were as harmless as they appeared, why did the girls get so excited? Surely there was something, well, *sinister* in all that . . .

Truth to tell, an enormous amount of the Beatles' appeal had nothing to do with music. The facts that they were young, rather cuddly-looking, and had a talent for smart-aleck remarks and absurdity, explained much of their appeal. They mocked ostentation in society, in themselves, and even in their fans. At live concerts, the girls squealed and shrieked so loudly and so continuously that the boys sometimes stopped singing into their mikes and just mouthed the words—and no one was the wiser.

Their tunes had much of the strong rhythm and lighthearted, tongue-in-cheek brashness that made rock 'n' roll popular in the first place. They sang covers of older rock 'n' roll songs by Chuck Berry and others, but they also sang their own material, which was often steeped in the centuries-old British folk-song tradition. Consider the song "Eleanor Rigby," for instance, which uses the ancient Dorian mode found so often in old British folk melodies. Another modal tune is "Norwegian Wood," which uses the Mixolydian mode.*

These qualities—together with lighthearted, sometimes frivolous (but often poetic) texts—were like a fresh breeze to a pop-music field that was stuck at the rock-abilly and rhythm-and-blues level. Rock has always changed rapidly, mostly because each style of rock tends to become a parody of itself so quickly. To a certain extent, such exaggeration is an element of rock's basic aesthetic. It is effective as satire; it loses force when it is taken seriously. In these early days, pomposity was a fault the Beatles easily avoided.

Beatle tunes (most of them written by John Lennon or Paul McCartney) usually have one musical idea that pervades and gives character to the whole song. In "Norwegian Wood" and "Eleanor Rigby," as mentioned above, it is their modalism. In "Yesterday," it is the bittersweet digression into the relative minor that occurs in the second measure, and also in the bridge, or release. "Got to Get You Into My Life," with its rubber-ball rhythm and energy, just wouldn't work without that upward jump of a seventh in the third measure. The examples could go on and on.

As the group matured and accepted the fact of their own enormous success, the Beatles began to reach out for new sources of ideas and inspiration. Curiously enough, one source was the classical-music tradition of India. George Harrison discovered the *sitar* and its best-known exponent in the West, Ravi Shankar. While he used the *sitar* as if it were some exotic version of the guitar, he at least introduced the sound of the instrument to a vast audience, and brought this fascinating musical tradition to the attention of Europe and America.

---

* You can play the Dorian mode on the piano by playing an octave scale, from D to D, using all white keys. To play the Mixolydian mode, play from G to G on the white keys.

The Beatle songs of the late 1960s changed from bubble-gum confections like "I Want to Hold Your Hand" to more mature topics (as in the song, "Strawberry Fields Forever") and much more adventurous musical resources. Besides the occasional use of the *sitar*, they used electronic distortions of recorded sound, and on the "super-album" *Sergeant Pepper's Lonely Hearts Club Band* even used a symphony orchestra. As so often in rock, pomposity was once more rearing its head. Yet out of these experiments in blending rock with the music of the symphony hall or of other cultures grew one of the most interesting and significant styles in the history of popular music—a subject we shall discuss in later chapters. After 1970, the Beatles broke up and pursued solo careers. In December 1980 John Lennon, the foremost songwriter of the four, was assassinated by a deranged fan.

Other British Groups

Once the Beatles had broken the American ice, a deluge of British bands followed in their wake. One group that had brief popular success was the Dave Clark Five (DC 5). The group specialized in loose-jointed, danceable music with no particular message. The message of "no-message" was well received; the group made at least a dozen appearances on Ed Sullivan's popular TV variety show.

Aside from the Beatles, the other "monster" British group was the self-proclaimed "Greatest Rock 'n' Roll Band in the World," the Rolling Stones. In many ways, the Stones were the dark counterpart of the winsome, witty Beatles. From the beginning, their image was strident, theatrical, and violent. They carried sexual innuendo to the point of an outright proposition ("Let's Spend the Night Together," the title of one song, was tempered down to "Let's Spend Some Time Together" for an appearance on Ed Sullivan's show). Stories of drug-taking and trashed hotel rooms trailed behind the Stones like a brown smog. At the Altamont concert in 1969, the notorious Hell's Angels motorcycle gang, who were there to "protect" the Rolling Stones from their fans, stabbed a man to death and beat others with pool cues. It wasn't the Stones' fault, of course, but it was the sort of incident that checkered their career.

The Rolling Stones appealed mostly to people who liked their rock raw and explicit. Perhaps inspired by the *Sergeant Pepper* album, Mick Jagger and Company made a lavishly expensive record entitled *Their Satanic Majesties Request*. In this album, the Stones experimented with some of the arty musical devices explored in the Beatles' album. The fans objected strenuously, however, and the Rolling Stones have been basic rock 'n' rollers ever since.

The story does not quite end there, however. These efforts at dressing up rock in the trappings of art music, while tentative and rather crudely conceived, had important consequences within a short while. These consequences came about, and reached their highest peak, in the works of British rock groups. These early Beatles and Rolling Stones efforts led to some really interesting musical developments, which will be described at length in later chapters.

Like the Dave Clark Five, Herman's Hermits intended their music to be danceable and fun. Herman, whose real name was Peter Noone, expressed a dislike for the outrageous and exhibitionistic trends in rock. The group had a strong country-and-western flavor in its performances, and, like the DC 5, rolled up an impressive number of best-selling records.

At the opposite pole of rock, the Animals, and their successors, Eric Burdon and the New Animals, were closer to the Rolling Stones' style. Their bluesy, candid-about-sex songs and onstage antics suggested the appropriateness of the group's name.

One group might be counted as a British rock band, even though we usually think of them as Australian. The Brothers Gibb, or the Bee Gees, began their musical careers in Australia, but they were born in Manchester, an industrial city located in north central England, not far from the Beatles' native Liverpool. The Bee Gees for a time became one of the more permanent and successful fixtures in the field of rock.

Other English rock groups have attained at least modest celebrity on this side of the Atlantic. The quiet, satirical duo of Chad (Stuart) and Jeremy (Clyde) explored the terrain to be thoroughly conquered by Americans Simon and Garfunkel. The Hollies took their name from American rocker Buddy Holly. Several groups, such as the Incredible String Band, followed the Beatles into Hindu philosophy and the use of non-Western instruments such as the Indian *sitar*, the Islamic *oud*, and the less exotic American banjo. Guitar virtuoso Jimi Hendrix (raised in America, but first popular in England) drew acclaim for his brilliant playing, but became perhaps more famous for setting his guitars on fire on stage.

The Who, whose "rock opera," *Tommy*, is a landmark in the trend toward fusing rock with other musical forms, also gained a reputation for "destructo-rock." Elton John, who played the role of the Pinball Wizard in the film version of *Tommy*, has made his incredible collection of incredible eyeglasses his trademark. Eric Clapton headed Cream, an aggressive, blues-based group that borrowed from avant-garde jazz the concept of simultaneous soloing by all the group's members.

England also produced single vocalists of prominence. Dusty Springfield (Mary Catherine O'Brien) is probably best remembered for songs from films, notably "The Look of Love," from *Casino Royale*. Lulu sang "To Sir With Love," the title song from the Sidney Poitier film. Petula Clark, whose style placed her firmly in the pop category, had the good fortune to record songs by the vastly talented Tony Hatch, among others. His song "Downtown," perhaps Pet's best-known single, is a sophisticated masterpiece of compositional craftsmanship. Welshman Tom Jones briefly became a sex symbol as well as a popular singer in the later 1960s.

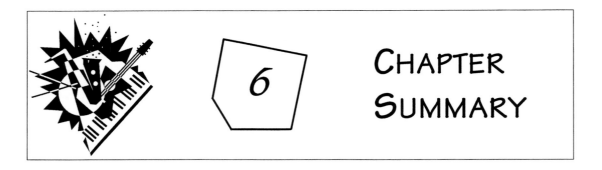

CHAPTER SUMMARY

The initial wave of rock 'n' roll surged outward from the United States in the 1950s. In the early 1960s, it washed back to our shores, especially from England. The crest of the wave was the Beatles, but many other groups followed.

What came back was a modified form of rock, strong in rhythm, but with a lyricism that borrowed from English folk music. Soon, too, the experiments with "symphonic" or "art" rock began, and exotic instruments like the *sitar* and the *oud* found their way into recordings, along with accompanying symphony orchestras. These experiments were forecasts of an exciting new type of music to come.

Rock's vulgar, exhibitionistic side also found expression in British rock. Performers and groups ranging from Jimi Hendrix to the Rolling Stones found a steady and enthusiastic audience for their strutting and instrument smashing, as well as for their music. Their fans liked their music loud, strong, and raunchy, with a strong visual element. To them, singers like Petula Clark were too effete to merit consideration. Thus, rock had split into different schools by 1965: Some fans wanted only hard, heavy rock 'n' roll, others preferred a tamer, more sophisticated brand of rock. This fracturing into schools continued and accelerated during the next decade. All sorts of hyphenated forms—folk-rock, acid rock, techno-rock, jazz-rock—appeared complete with an international audience. Before we consider these, however, we should consider a development in the American pop-music scene—the California Sound.

LISTENING GUIDE 1: "Long Dark Road," by the Hollies. From *The Hollies' Greatest Hits*, Epic PE3206 l.

<u>Description.</u> An introduction played on acoustic guitars leads to a verse sung solo and repeated in two-part harmony. A break featuring harmonica is followed by the chorus, based on the text of the title, which is sung in long note values and backed by a gospel-style organ. This is followed by a harmonica solo. We hear the chorus again, sung with a counterpoint by part of the group. The verse appears again, sung solo, and is followed by the counterpointed chorus, which is repeated as the song fades.

<u>Analysis.</u> The Hollies, a group named for early rock 'n' roll star Buddy Holly, originated in Manchester, England, near Liverpool (as their accents suggest). They

were one of the most consistently successful rock groups in England, though their appeal in America never approached that of the Beatles or the Stones.

The harmonica, the prevalence of acoustic instruments, and the five-voice vocal harmonies are all characteristic of the Hollies. The sound smacks of early rock 'n' roll, strongly flavored with black gospel style. The song is a simple one, involving only two phrases, which are very different from each other. The texture varies from solo to five-part ensemble singing in a pattern typical of popular songs—from thin (solo) through gradually thicker (duet) to dense harmonies to harmonized counterpoint. The harmonica and the organ give a folk-gospel quality to the song, which merits the description "blue-eyed soul"—that is, a white version of black soul music.

LISTENING GUIDE 2:   "Baby, You're a Rich Man," by the Beatles. From *Magical Mystery Tour,* Capitol 2835.

Description.   The piece opens with a "chug-chuga-chug" rhythm that continues through the entire composition. This is quickly followed by noodlings on an instrument that sounds like an Indian *shenai*. The vocal that appears next is done in high tenor voices, followed by a solo ("What do you want to be?"). The volume swells as if going on to another idea, but instead, there is a repetition of the previous vocal ideas. Eventually, the crescendo does lead to a new section, in which the title line of the song is virtually shouted, with handclaps on beats two and four of each measure.

The next section is a virtual clone of the above, with different words to the verses, and occasional noodlings by the odd instrument. The song ends on a "radio-station fade" based on the song's title.

Analysis.   This piece represents the Beatles when they were trying more elaborate production and instrumental effects. The basic format, however, is still fundamental Beatles—pronounced rhythm, simple structure, a great deal of repetition, and a song text that seems mocking and cynical, while being naive at the same time.

7 SURF'S UP!

Here's a little association game for you: what do all the following have in common: John Muir; Rudolph Valentino; Marilyn Monroe; Ronald Reagan; Tinsel Town; Sunkist; Gallo wines; Tournament of Roses; Death Valley; Grauman's Chinese Theater; Steve Young.

You got it (didn't you?). All of the above are closely associated with California, a state of mind as much as it is a state of the Union. Consider the images that the name California brings to mind. John Sutter's mill, and the shiny pebbles in the millrace. The Golden Gate Bridge, with squat Alcatraz grim in the distance. Faye Wray and her furry admirer. Yosemite Valley, with brooding Half Dome towering above Camp Curry. Palm Springs and Malibu and Monterey. *Streets of San Francisco* and *Beverly Hills 90210* and *L.A. Law*. Mountain climbing and trail hiking and splendid skiing and . . .

And surfing. Sooner or later, the subject of surfing is bound to crop up. All those lithe, golden-tanned athletic bodies hanging ten just under the curl of a great Pacific boomer, darting like water beetles into the clear just before the wave collapses and gulps them up like super-Jaws. For millions of landlocked, envious teens around the world, surfboarding seems a promise of summer, good times, and youth without end.

In the early 1960s, sun-baked, sprawling Los Angeles—"Los Anneles" to the natives—was home to the Wilson family, whose three boys—Brian, Dennis, and Carl—were in high school. The three were amateur musicians who enjoyed singing songs in harmony at friends' houses and family get-togethers, often with their cousin, Al Jardine. The group was good enough to sing and play at high-school dances, first as Carl and the Passions, later as Kenny and the Cadets. Sounds like a thousand other bands in a thousand other towns, right?

Well, yes—except that the Wilson boys were onto something extraordinary. Chiefly through the efforts of Brian, who had taken a course in music theory, the group began writing and performing songs about the southern California lifestyle, and especially about the popular teen pastime of riding surfboards on the Pacific's huge, thundering breakers. Blending elements of jazz, pop, and rock 'n' roll, and treating their songs with slick, tight performances, the group exploded on the popular music scene as the originators of what was called the California Sound.

The Wilson brothers, plus Al Jardine and Mike Love, first recorded an original song, "Surfin'," for Candix Records, a Los Angeles company, in 1961. We'll buy your record, said the representative from Candix. Now, what shall we call your group? After some discussion, they adopted the name the Beach Boys, and so they have been ever since. Soon Candix sold their hot new property to massive Capitol Records, and the Beach Boys became an instant national phenomenon.

Brian Wilson's newly discovered talents as a composer led to hit after hit— "Surfin' Safari" in 1962, their first nationwide monster hit; "Surfin' USA" in 1963; "Surfer Girl" and the new hot-rod songs, like "Little Deuce Coupe," "Fun, Fun, Fun," "Little Honda," and "I Get Around." In the mid-1960s, the Beach Boys stood astride the popular-music field like some sun-soaked outtake from *American Grafitti*, flushed with success after success. They portrayed a never-never land of perpetual summer, fast cars, and two girls for every boy.

Having created the California Sound, Brian Wilson and Company shared it with their friends—specifically, Jan (Berry) and Dean (Torrance). These two fellow Angelenos sometimes sang and played backup guitar with the Wilsons, and many of their hit songs ("Surf City," "Drag City," and the prophetic "Dead Man's Curve" among them) were written in collaboration with Brian Wilson. Friends since junior high school, Jan and Dean played on the same varsity football team in high school. Like the Wilsons, they were good-looking, tanned, athletic blonds with all-American grins.

Musically, the characteristics of the Beach Boys and Jan and Dean were nearly identical. The songs were bubbly blendings of rockabilly beat with close, jazz-flavored harmonizations modeled on the style of the Hi Los or the Four Freshmen. Added to this, the lead singer played off against riffing contrapuntal lines sung by other members of the group. The top voice sang in a reedy falsetto, and extra parts were created in the studio by overdubbing. This technical trickery is achieved by making a tape recording of, say, the electric guitar part and one singer. This tape is then combined with a second tape of a rhythm guitar and a singer doing a harmony part. The process is continued until the desired texture and balance is achieved, layer on layer. Many of the Beach Boys/Jan and Dean tracks involved the use of much over-dubbing.

You can check out some of these characteristics by listening to some examples. Listen first to "Surfin' USA," by the Beach Boys. The song opens with a springy beat and a classic, 1950s rock 'n' roll introduction by the instruments. This is followed by the verse, sung in a relaxed manner, with other voices chording on "oo-oo" in the background. On the next verse, introduced by a drum break, the backups sing a riff ("Inside, outside . . .") behind the lead singers. These two verses alternate again, and then an organ and guitar swap halves of a verse in solos. The song then spins out into a radio-station fade on the last line of the song. This evocation of the surfing scene lasts just under two and a half minutes.

Turn now to Jan and Dean's "Drag City." The song begins with the sound of revving engines, then breaks into a unison verse setting the story line. This, in turn, is followed by a chorus set to a blues chord progression, with elaborate overdubbing (remember, we are hearing only *two* singers). The melody is set against a falsetto "oo-oo" riff, ending with a harmonized invocation to "bum up the quarter-mile" drag strip. The song makes a surprise modulation, and verse and chorus repeat, this time with a backup riff on the verse as well as the chorus. The piece ends with an overlapping set of riffs. This is technically and musically a complex composition, with a large number of effects crammed into its two and a quarter minutes.

Between them, these two songs typify the California Sound, which in the mid-1960s challenged the British Sound of the Beatles. On the part of the Beach Boys, at least, the challenge was a conscious one. Brian Wilson, who served as producer of their records as well as star composer, felt the pressure of keeping up with the Moptops, as the shaggy-haired Beatles were nicknamed. When the British band released *Revolver* and, later, *Sergeant Pepper's Lonely Hearts Club Band*—two experimental recordings with enlarged themes and scope—Brian attempted some experiments of his own in response.

Somehow, though, the chemistry wasn't right. Beatles fans accepted the sound of the Indian *sitar* in their music with good grace, if not enthusiasm; but when the Beach Boys featured a Japanese *koto* on their album, *Pet Sounds*, their American audience stayed away by the thousands. The rejection hurt Brian Wilson, who, for all his sun-and-fun lyrics, was actually introverted and moody. He threw himself into a second projected album, to be called *Smile*, but his personal problems intensified, the production of *Smile* finally collapsed, and Brian had a nervous breakdown and took refuge in LSD.

Pieces of the *Smile* album finally appeared in a new album called *Smiley Smile*, but critics panned this recording, also. What the fans really wanted, it seemed, was more surfers-and-dragsters songs. Brian gradually fought his way back from his problems, but never became the dominating creative force he had once been. He contributed three or four songs each to succeeding albums, which returned to the California formula, but his brother Carl wrote many of the new songs. Since the late 1970s, the Beach Boys have basically been a touring group, singing the old songs to fans old and new, highly successful, but no longer a protean force in popular music. The drowning death of Dennis Wilson in December 1983 cast a pall over the Minstrels of Eternal Youth, a jarring, somber note that makes their songs more bittersweet.

Before passing on from the Beach Boys, however, we should sum up their contributions to popular music. First, the group elevated the standards of production that the listening audience would accept by their meticulous work in getting everything just right. "Good Vibrations," for example, their smash hit of 1966, took six months and dozens of overdubs to create. Some of their later recorded work depended on studios so completely that they could not be done in concert as they sounded on the record.

Second, the Beach Boys spotlighted California as a world-renowned center for creative popular music. Their concern for musical tightness and careful production are characteristics of more recent southern California groups such as Steely Dan. While they were scarcely forerunners of such West Coast groups as Jefferson Airplane and the Grateful Dead, their popularity did focus attention on the region, and thus made the successes of others easier.

Third, the Beach Boys helped elevate the musical standards of rock. In the work of Brian Wilson and others, popular music took long strides away from the three-chord R & B simplicity of earlier work, and began to demand better technique and greater sophistication of its performers. Surfing songs celebrated good times and long summers, but they also made basic changes in the sound of popular music.

The summers ended all too quickly for Jan and Dean, though. Riding the crest of their popularity on hit after hit, they seemed to epitomize the songs they sang. Jan Berry had dreams of becoming a doctor, and Dean Torrance could indulge his strong interest in graphic arts. Then, one April night in 1966, Jan was in a car wreck that left him paralyzed for over a year. Despite attempts at comebacks, Jan has never been able to succeed as a performer since then. Ironically, the accident took place not long after they recorded one of their big hot-rod hits, "Dead Man's Curve," about a stretch of California highway famous for its auto wrecks.

CHAPTER SUMMARY

7

Surfing music rose, crested, and then crashed like a great Pacific roller, strewing hit songs and bubbly, talented performers like sea foam on the beach. The basic problem was that the songs dealt with superficial concerns—surfing, fast cars—and so had no way to achieve a lasting place in popular music. The additional burden of tragic endings for some of the performers added a somber coda to the music of eternal fun. The surf-singers did leave a permanent mark on pop music, however, in the well-crafted arrangements and the elaborate, painstaking production they pioneered. The fad of surf music ebbed quickly, but the efforts of the performers continue to affect popular music.

Suggested Projects

1. The Beach Boys became nationally popular a generation ago. Do their songs relate to young people of today? Are surfing and fast cars still popular subjects with teens? What sorts of topics might appeal to more modern audiences? Discuss these questions with other members of your class. Perhaps you might want to try writing lyrics for modern songs.

2. Compare a Beach Boys recording with one by the Beatles from the same period. What musical similarities can you hear? What musical differences do you notice?

3. In the mid-1960s, certain rock groups began using non-Western instruments such as the *sitar* and the *koto* in popular music. Write a one-page report on each of these instruments.

Suggested Records

Recordings of any of the artists mentioned may be used to illustrate their individual styles.

8 THE FOLK MOVEMENT

Imagine for a moment that electronic communications didn't exist. Think first about taking motion pictures out of your life; no *Star Wars*, no *Close Encounters*. Next, banish television—news, sitcoms, cop shows, MTV, all gone. Swallow hard, and eliminate radio as well. Poof, no Walkman, no "box," no Top Forty, no deejays. Chuck out the telephone as well, a minor inconvenience if you have survived the previous traumas. What's left?

What's left is whatever amusement you can provide yourself, or attend in person. What's left is Grandpa Joe playing polkas on his squeeze-box, or Uncle Ned picking his guitar and singing cowboy ballads, or Cousin Minnie batting out "I Want a Girl Just Like the Girl that Married Dear Old Dad" on the tinny old upright. Liven this scenario with an occasional church social, a concert by a touring company, or the town band playing in the park for the volunteer fire company's annual fundraiser. This is just about how things were when the twentieth century got under way—not that long ago, when you think about it.

Entertainment in the years before electronics was limited to what you could provide yourself or attend in person. That meant that the average quality was probably much lower than today. Maybe Uncle Ned was the best ballad singer you knew, but by professional standards, he might have been pretty awful. Anyway, you could only hear first-rate performances on those rare occasions when you could go to a live presentation. Even a moderately good performance must have sounded thrilling and exciting.

How different things are now! We are swamped, deluged, saturated with music from twenty different radio stations, all playing the same hundred or so tunes day in, day out, simply because we can't create new songs fast enough to feed the insatiable market. We stroll to music, we socialize to music, we buy groceries to it, we sing along with it, we talk over it, we study to it. Music is as much a part of our environment as the air we breathe—and, like the air, we tend to take it for granted, to ignore it, to use it as background for other things we do. At a time when the world's finest performers are at everyone's command, most people treat those performers as sonic stuffing.

Even the old, traditional music—the polkas and the cowboy ballads and the pop tunes of another era—has a hard time getting the audience's attention. Unless you have a special interest in, say, Dixieland jazz or Child ballads, you tend to ignore them when you hear them. Uncle Ned's version of "The Streets of Laredo" got respect from all his audience in 1910, but if we heard a recording of Waylon Jennings singing it today, only the country-and-western buffs would be apt to stay tuned.

With all of this new, *new*, NEW music constantly being dinned into people's ears, one might wonder how in the world a folk-music revival ever got started in the 1960s. It's a good question, and the answer is not a simple one. It is based much more on the social and economic climate of the period than it is on purely musical circumstances. Let's touch base with a few of these causes of the folk—and folk-rock—phenomenon.

Causes of the Folk Revival

For one thing, after more than a generation of radio and phonograph, most young people had lost touch with the old folk music of Europe. To them, the ancient ballads their grandparents knew were new and different from the music with which they were familiar. Popular music had become the folk music of their generation.

A second cause of the folk-music revival was the explosion in the number of college students that began after World War II, as ex-GI's used their government benefits to attend degree-granting institutions. This explosion began in the late 1940s, and continued through the 1960s. This new generation of children of the ex-GI's had been taught to pursue their interests and to seek relevance in their studies. Many of them found, to their delight, that the songs of their ancestors often dealt with topics—love, disappointment, work, war—that had meaning for them, too. They took courses in folk music, and they went to coffeehouses in the evenings to hear folk singers. As often as not, they also learned to strum a guitar and sing the ballads of their forebears themselves.

The social situation of the 1960s was a third cause of the interest in folk music. Those years were turbulent, even revolutionary, for some—even though they were placid and carefree for many others. Two great social movements overlapped: the push for universal civil rights, and the opposition to the unpopular Vietnam War. These, in turn, affected a multitude of other causes—the War on Poverty, the Free Speech Movement, the American Indian Movement, and on and on. Antiwar songs from the past, such as "Johnny Has Gone for a Soldier" and "All Quiet Along the Potomac Tonight," were sung with new enthusiasm by opponents of America's Southeast Asian commitment. At almost the same time, the civil rights partisans revived songs from the rich, black gospel repertoire to foster unity and to symbolize their ideas.

For these reasons and more, students in the sixties found the old folk-song literature full of new meaning for them. They studied and sang the old songs with enthusiasm, adding modern touches as they did. By good fortune (and governmental foresight), many of these songs had been recorded by authentic performers during the 1930s and 1940s through a federal project to help the nation climb out of the Great Depression. These recordings, edited and published by the Library of Congress (or LC, as it is often known), are still available, and form a priceless record of music and folk tales from early America.

Folk-Rock Style

It is a rule of musical scholarship that it is always dangerous to talk about a "style" of music. It's too easy to find examples that don't fit the style. The rule applies especially in the case of what we are calling folk-rock or the folk movement. Can you lump Pete Seeger and the Mamas and the Papas together? How about Simon and Garfunkel, Bob Dylan, Joan Baez, and Buffy Sainte-Marie? Why would Donovan be in, but the Beatles ("Eleanor Rigby," "Yellow Submarine") be out?

It may help if we distinguish the style from both the viewpoint of the folk traditionalist and that of the rock 'n' roller. The folk roots of the style can be seen quite often in the songs themselves. Pete and Peggy Seeger, Joan Baez, Burl Ives, and many others perform mostly authentic folk material—the Child and broadside ballads, work and labor-union songs, and the folk-like songs of Woody Guthrie, for example. Even the composed songs, such as Bob Dylan's "Blowin' in the Wind" or "It Ain't Me, Babe," contain the diatonic melodies and primary chords so common in folk music.

Folk style is evident in the manner of singing, too. Listen to Pete Seeger (whose father, Charles Seeger, had a lot to do with those LC recordings) perform in his nasal tenor. Compare that with the sound of Elvis Presley, whose voice mixed elements of both Huddie Ledbetter and Bing Crosby. Seeger's is an uncultivated voice; he's not trying to sound good, whatever that word might mean. Or compare Joan Baez with, say, Janis Joplin. Joan's voice is usually pure, true, a bit chesty at times; Janis works to get a lot of black vocal effects, such as growls, glisses, or shouts. Similarly, B.B. King sings in an authentically black style; Charlie Pride has mastered another culture's style.

It won't do to push authenticity too far. Compare, if you can, some of the white folk singers on the LC recordings with Pete Seeger, and you should notice one major difference. The singers on the LC records simply sing a story, with little expression of personal feelings. Seeger's delivery is emotional; he tells his tale with drama and concern. If you can find an old Carter Family recording and compare it with one of Peter, Paul, and Mary, the same difference will be obvious.

Two factors help explain this difference. First, to the old folk performers, the story was the important thing, not the performance. The folk singers (in Anglo-American culture) were a sort of audible magazine. They told the story with as little feeling as a book's print would have. The folk-revival singers are more interested in giving the audience the emotional message of the song. The college kids in the coffeehouses could read the songs for themselves; the singers tried to bring the cold print to emotional life. The second factor in this difference in performance is that white singers in this century have been greatly influenced by black music and performance. Emotion is the essence of black folk singing and blues singing. This has increasingly influenced white singers as well.

Finally, the folk movement can be identified by the kinds of instruments used. Banjos and acoustic guitars carry the main accompaniment load, with an occasional dulcimer used for special effect. In folk-rock, one may hear a drum set as well. The amplified strings of rock are usually missing, or tuned down.

Performers

Although the era of folk-rock was brief, its influence spread like ripples on a pond throughout much of the rock scene to come. Pete Seeger represented the traditional folk musicians of the period. He expressed his concern for environmental preservation in traditional songs and ballads, strumming banjo or guitar in concerts that drew thousands of supporters. His female counterparts were sister Peggy Seeger and Joan Baez.

Bob Dylan (nee Bob Zimmerman) occupies a central place in the evolution of rock since the mid-1960s, mostly because of the expressive songs he has written. His strong melodies and folk-like harmonies celebrated the current enthusiasms of many young people, from racial equality ("Blowin' in the Wind") to antiwar sentiment ("Masters of War") to drug experimentation ("Mr. Tambourine Man"). His career has been a fitful one, with periods of great popularity alternating with times when he has withdrawn completely from public life.

Other folk and folk-rock singles of note rode the brief wave as well. Scotsman Donovan Leitch wrote some gentle ballads and flirted with both avant-garde rock and the writing of film scores. Judy Collins, a classically trained pianist with strong political convictions, continues a varied career as composer, performer, and arranger. Her arrangement of the old hymn "Amazing Grace" achieved surprising hit status. Phil Ochs attained brief renown, chiefly for his antiwar songs. Buffy Sainte-Marie stressed her Cree Indian heritage in her song material.

Several groups also flourished at the peak of the era. The New Christy Minstrels revived in their name, and to some extent in their music, one of the most popular groups (the Christy Minstrels) of the previous century. Well-known vocal trios included the Kingston Trio, the Chad Mitchell Trio, and the lush-harmonied Peter, Paul, and Mary—whose arrangements, like those of the Beach Boys, borrowed from jazz groups such as the Four Freshmen. The meteoric Mamas and the Papas streaked to stardom and stayed there for three brief years, from 1965 through 1967, before dissolving in 1968.

We have already mentioned the eruption of California groups onto the national stage in the chapter on surfing music. Another side of California appeared in the folk-rock group called the Byrds. One of the central personalities of this changeable ensemble was Roger (nee Jim) McGuinn, who played guitar and sang. The group has variously recorded as a quintet, a quartet, and a trio, and has changed styles frequently. David Crosby, later famous in combination with Stephen Stills and Graham Nash, was one of the original Byrds.

Folk Movement Contributions

Folk-rock, as such, had a very brief run as a nationwide phenomenon. It sprang to life in the mid-sixties, and faded in the early seventies, a time span paralleling the Vietnam War protests with which folk-rock was so closely connected. Many of the personalities, and most of the groups, involved in folk-rock either receded in popularity or vanished altogether.

The influence of this brief but fertile movement has extended far beyond its own borders, however. Let's trace some of its effects on the larger rock scene. Perhaps the greatest influence of folk-rock can be found in the intellectual interests and sophistication of its audience. The college youngsters who listened to Joan Baez or the Mamas and the Papas were not mainly interested in body music. They listened for the message of the words, and they critiqued the music with a wider knowledge of musical possibilities. The times, they were a-changin', and the music was, too.

Folk-rock also continued the trend away from three-chord harmonic simplicity. Much of the folk repertoire calls for harmonies based on the ancient modes—Aeolian, Dorian, and Mixolydian especially. A performer who could only manage G, C, and D7 would be unable to play a lot of new songs.

Interest in Euro-American folk music led to interest in the folk and classical music of other countries as well. The "discovery" of Indian classical music by the Beatles and others led to brief "raga-rock" experiments, which were carried much further by people like guitarist John McLaughlin and others. We will discuss these fascinating developments in later chapters.

After a decade (1953-63) of exploring the combination of R & B and bluegrass, and focusing on danceable beat and extravagant appearance, rock turned to other old sources for new inspiration. The British groups added English accents and traditions to a basically Middle American genre. The Californians picked up some of jazz's slick harmonies and big-band effects. The folk performers expanded the repertoire, lowered the volume, and raised the intellectual content of rock. Each new style added a layer to rock's gaudy, glitzy, outrageous cake. There were other movements afoot during the fertile sixties as well, and some became caught up and identified with the dark, ugly, spreading stain of drug use. This style became known as acid rock, and we'll discuss it in the next chapter.

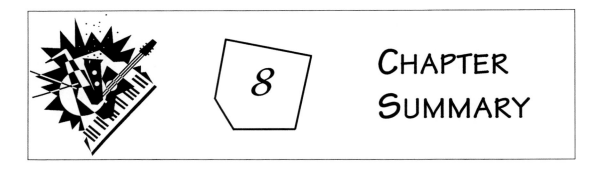

CHAPTER SUMMARY

8

Where one generation sneered at hillbilly music, their sons and daughters in the 1960s found new inspiration in ballads and spirituals from the past. The young enthusiasts had their own ideas about how the songs should be performed, however. The songs now should be sung with expression and emotional commitment, and the instrumental backing should be rich and full and professionally played. New, folk-like songs joined the old repertoire and composer-performers like Donovan and Buffy Sainte-Marie and Bob Dylan were enormously popular. Folk-rock introduced a rather novel concept into the larger field of rock, namely, the idea that songs were to be *thought about* rather than just *danced to*. The ramifications of this radical idea were, for some, far-reaching.

Suggested Projects

1. See if you can find two recordings of the same folk song, one sung by Pete Seeger or Joan Baez, the other from an LC or Folkways folk recording. Compare the performances in terms of style of voice used, instrumental accompaniment, and the words to the song. Which version do you prefer, and why?

2. Write a two-page or longer report on either the Child ballads or the broadside ballads. Include information about the age of each as a repertoire, the subject matter, the type of musical setting, and the appearance of the same songs in the United States.

3. The folk movement in popular music gained much of its impetus from the antiwar sentiment of the late sixties. If we were to have a folk revival today, one of the topics of protest songs might well be protection of the environment. What songs of popular performers in the past few years deal with ecology and the environment? Make a list, and quote sections of the texts of the songs. You may find them in surprising places.

Suggested Records

Baez, Joan. *The Country Music Album.* (2 rec.) Vanguard T105, Tl06.

Byrds, The. *Original Singles, 1965–67.* Columbia FC 37335E.

Seeger, Peggy, and Ewan McColl. *Kilroy Was Here.* Folkways 8562.

Seeger, Pete. *Sing Along.* (2 rec.) Folkways FXM-36055.

9 ETCHED IN ACID

A shy young man meets a beautiful girl and falls helplessly in love. However, she hardly notices him, and spurns his attentions. He becomes despondent and decides to end his life with narcotics. The drug dosage is too weak to kill him, however, and he only falls into a stupor, in which he has horrifying dreams. He dreams that he kills his love, and is convicted of murder. He seems to witness his own execution. Finally, at his funeral, a band of demons and monsters hold a wild revel, led by none other than the girl he loved, transformed into a witch.

The plot for a new horror flick? A soap opera based on *Night of the Living Dead?* Neither. This is a brief sketch of the story line of the *Sinfonie Fantastique*, written in 1830 by Hector Berlioz. The problem of young people and drugs—and bad trips—is hardly a new one.

In parts of Europe in the 1820s, just as in parts of the United States in the 1960s, a permissive attitude toward morals and drug-taking prevailed, and some people had money enough to buy whatever they pleased. Wealth seems to give rise to permissiveness; too much money and too little control often go together. It was probably inevitable that those who lived the rich and exaggerated lifestyle of rock performers should try the ultimate exaggeration of life—hard drugs.

Drugs were unfortunately a common hazard of certain other musicians' lives as well. Such jazz giants as Charlie Parker and Stan Getz fought battles with heroin. Early rockers modeled their language ("cool," "boppin'"), their dress, and their behavior on some of the more colorful jazz personalities. Drug-taking, unfortunately, was part of the package.

The main difference was that, in San Francisco in the mid-1960s, the argument was seriously advanced by influential people that getting stoned was somehow *good* for you. The recent invention of lysergic acid diethylamide (LSD), a powerful and unpredictable mind-distorting drug, was viewed by some as heralding a new, Aquarian age of peace and love. Acid, as LSD was commonly called, left no needle tracks in arms, needed no cooking, was almost never lethal, and could be slipped into the prom punch for a lark with little chance of getting caught. Of course, on the negative side, it did make some people psychotic . . .

Portly Tom Donahue, his broad spade beard streaked with gray, was one of San Francisco's most prominent disc jockeys at the beginning of the 1960s. Then he discovered acid, and experienced its mind-warping psychedelic capabilities. He decided that turning on had a real future. He quit his job and invested in a psychedelic nightclub and an FM station that would play rock by local bands, avoiding the Top-Forty format and seeking to express psychedelia in music.

He found some groups ready at hand, groups that preferred the laid-back, zonked-out hippie aesthetic popular at that time to the well-scrubbed exuberance of the Beach Boys or the terribly serious social involvement of the folkies. Such groups took a casual approach to rehearsing, and their personnel seldom joined the Musicians' Union. Their native haunts were small clubs with tripped-out clientele where one could get high on the marijuana smoke in the air alone.

At first the repertoire of these groups tended toward traditional rock 'n' roll and folk group covers. Some of the performers were college kids out for fun; others were amateur musicians looking for a few bucks and fewer responsibilities. They named their bands things like the Final Solution or the Great Society or Big Brother and the Holding Company. None of them, most likely, had any serious thoughts of fame and fortune.

Big Daddy Donahue undertook to give these groups radio time, and soon the style some called the San Francisco Sound began to jell. It wasn't just dance music, such as all of previous rock 'n' roll had been. It was also drug music. The words of the songs harped over and over on the mystical-muzzy, spaced-out, psychotic glories of being stoned into insensibility. The ambience of the music—at first folksy, featuring acoustic instruments like guitar and harmonica, with lots of multiple jamming—suited small clubs and individualistic performers.

The sound and the songs were novel and different enough to have commercial appeal in some quarters. It wasn't long before any number of groups began exploiting the new style, and recording companies began signing bands to contracts. One of the first groups to record was Quicksilver Messenger Service, whose personnel changed rapidly over their rather short existence. Others soon sprang into the market—Moby Grape, the Grateful Dead, the Jefferson Airplane (later Starship), Country Joe and the Fish, the Steve Miller Band. By this time, the groups' records were being distributed nationwide. Most of the groups tightened up their performances (except possibly the Grateful Dead, who were known to spend half an hour tuning up and deciding what song to play). The general level of proficiency improved as more professional musicians exploited the market. Acid rock had arrived.

To understand how and why acid rock evolved, it's important to comprehend the social climate of the time. Our country was developing many noisy and vehement pressure groups—for civil rights, against the Vietnam War, and for or against dozens of other causes. The nation's time-honored customs and values were being successfully challenged, and a host of new challenges—justified or silly, valid or frivolous—were being raised. In a society where all traditional values are questioned, a popular music that preaches that Dope Is Good For You finds plenty of followers.

The music also collected ideologues of other stripes. Country Joe MacDonald had been a folk singer, especially of protest songs. With his new band, The Fish, he took to wearing protest buttons at concerts and keeping close touch with the student radicals at the University of California at Berkeley, one of the centers of dissidents in the late sixties. The Jefferson Airplane gradually evolved into the chief musical representative of the so-called counter-culture.

By 1966, the acid bands were regular features at San Francisco's Fillmore Ballroom, a young people's dance hall. Personnel from the various bands joined or started other groups almost weekly. Skip Spence, for example, who was the original drummer for the Jefferson Airplane, dropped out to help found the short-lived Moby Grape. The Airplane, in turn, added Grace Slick from the recently defunct Great Society. David Freiberg, an original with Quicksilver Messenger Service, eventually wound up with the Jefferson Starship.

The sound of the bands changed, too. Instead of the loose, loopy jamming of the earlier doper bands, the sound of most representative bands in 1969 had hardened considerably. Most instruments were electrically amplified, and the volume had been increased to the level of pain. Some groups added strobe lights to increase the psychedelic effect. The music—roaring-loud, distorted, repetitious—was a sonic approximation of what it was like to be on LSD, with all one's senses overloaded and the room and the people turned into melting Silly Putty.

Actually, the San Francisco Sound is not described so easily, because the many bands strove for different sounds. Most of the groups, however, used sound distortion, by inducing feedback in the amplifiers or even by ripping the speaker cones in their amps. The long, improvised solos often used modal scales bowed from Indian classical music. These long jams were also a characteristic of most acid-rock groups.

As the 1970s began, the acid-rock movement gradually faded. Most of the groups changed their styles; some of them simply self-destructed. A few major groups or performers continued to hold the attention of rock fans around the world. The Jefferson Airplane continued to fly, even though its engines gave off ominous sputterings. A major talent emerged as Mexican guitarist Carlos Santana worked his way out of the blues bands and created a new psychedelic-Latin sound with his own group. Still another major personality came out of Big Brother and the Holding Company. This was the ill-starred blues singer, Janis Joplin. Janis's tortured personality made her vulnerable to the lifestyle of the acid rockers. She soared to fame in 1968, but was drawn to booze and drugs like a moth to a flame. She died in 1970 of a heroin overdose.

Far from California, another psychedelic superstar exploded in a nova of acclaim, then winked out as quickly and as tragically as Janis Joplin. Jimi Hendrix, the Seattle-born guitarist, began his musical career as a backup in various black rock 'n' roll bands, including Little Richard and the Isley Brothers. He gained prominence in England as the centerpiece of the Jimi Hendrix Experience. The Experience quickly became a European sensation, and Jimi and Company made plans to return to America. Through appearances and recordings, the Jimi Hendrix Experience rocketed to fame in the States, as well.

A phenomenal guitarist, Jimi taught his own generation new ways to play the instrument. He also explored the uses of tonal distortion possible on the electric guitar. Mike Bloomfield, guitarist with the Butterfield Blues Band, once said that after hearing Hendrix play, he was ready to quit the guitar in frustration. Unfortunately, Jimi is probably better remembered for some of his hot-dog antics, which included playing the guitar behind his back, picking it with his teeth, and ending a performance by smashing and burning his guitar.

The meteor flamed out in September 1970, less than a month before Janis Joplin. Hendrix died at the peak of his career of a barbiturate overdose. The happy, drug-soaked peace-and-love lifestyle was showing its dark and ugly roots.

One veteran of the psychedelic scene not only survived, but took a major step forward in establishing the rights of performers to insist on quality recording of their work. Steve Miller's group became so popular that he was able to insist on careful, painstaking production of his records. Previously, recording had been an often slap-dash affair controlled by record company people who tended to be engineers or marketing analysts, not musicians. Miller's victory has meant a great improvement in recording quality across the industry for pop and rock musicians.

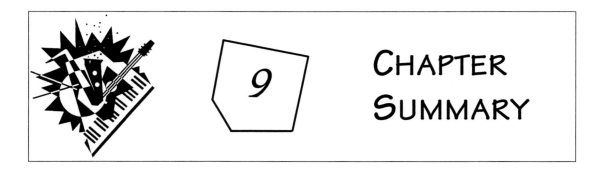

CHAPTER 9 SUMMARY

The 1960s and early 1970s were a period of social unrest and distortion, both here and around the world. Among the most distorted aspects of the period was the self-styled drug culture that sprang up, especially (in this country) in the San Francisco area. The foremost propagandists for the drug culture were the acid-rock bands. To create a musical analog for a drug trip, the groups evolved a sound that combined ear-damaging volume with massive electronic distortion and numbing repetition, topped off with blinking strobe lights or twirling mirror balls. Groups such as Jefferson Airplane/Starship and the Grateful Dead, and performers such as Janis Joplin and Jimi

Hendrix, extolled and exploited the psychedelic sound. More recent movements in rock, such as heavy metal, perpetuate many of the acid bands' characteristics.

Suggested Projects

1. Tom Donahue had a major influence on the success of the San Francisco bands. See if you can interview local radio personalities to get their thoughts on the influence disc jockeys have on the musical tastes of the local population. Perhaps you can contact people from a Top-Forty station, a country-and-western station, a gospel radio station, a funk-and-soul station, an easy-listening station, and a classical music station.

2. The tonal distortion of amplified instruments was a characteristic of the San Francisco sound. You may be able to experiment with some of these techniques. If you can get an amplifier and a microphone or electric guitar, try moving the mike or guitar closer to and further from the amp as you sing or play. If you can get some old speakers from a junked radio or TV, try ripping the paper cone and singing or playing through it. Could you use these sounds for expressive purposes?

3. Listen to several songs by the Jefferson Airplane or the Grateful Dead, and compare them to songs by either the Beach Boys or the Beatles. What do these songs have in common? What are the differences between them? Write a two- or three-page report on your findings.

Suggested Records

Grateful Dead. *Anthem of the Sun.* Warner Bros. 1749.

Hendrix, Jimi. *Free Spirit.* Accord SN 7112.

Jefferson Airplane. *The Worst of the Jefferson Airplane.* RCA AYL 1-3661.

Joplin, Janis. *I Got Dem Ol' Kozmic Blues Again Mama!* Columbia 9113.

Miller, Steve. *Fly Like an Eagle.* Mobile 021.

Santana, Carlos. *Abraxas.* Columbia HC 40130.

10 SOUL, MEMPHIS, MOTOWN, AND TSOP

Soul music is yearning music. It is the music of Blind Lemon Jefferson and his guitar telling us about how dark a night can be. It is the music of Johnny Dodds with his wailing, passionate clarinet answering Louis Armstrong. It is the sound of Ma Rainey recovering from a broken heart. It is the hoarse, gritty honesty of Bessie Smith belting out the blues in a voice that could rattle the windows in any nightclub in the country. Soul isn't exclusively black people's music—ever listen to Spanish gypsy songs?—but some of the best soul music came out of black American throats and hearts.

The term *soul music* became specifically attached to a style of black popular music during the 1960s. One of the most important figures in the spread of soul was James Brown. Like so many soul singers, Georgia-born Brown was raised on the country blues-and-gospel songs of the region. He began recording for a label based in Cincinnati, King Records, in 1956. By 1962 he was ready for a performance at the Apollo Theater in Harlem, an essential step in any black American performer's road to fame. In a time of rising black consciousness and pride, James Brown was acclaimed as Soul Brother Number One. The singer of "Say It Aloud—I'm Black and I'm Proud" expressed sentiments that millions of young black Americans were eager to hear.

If James Brown is Soul Brother Number One, number two can only be a fellow Georgian, Ray Charles. Blind since he was six, Ray evolved his singing and playing style out of the gospel singing of the rural South. Nowadays, his earthy, gravelly vocals are often backed by a slick band and the Raelettes, a female trio. Ray sings from his roots, tossing his head from side to side, stirring black and white listeners alike.

Still a third Georgian also developed into a major performer of soul music. This was Otis Redding, the first soul singer to gain widespread acceptance with white audiences. Otis's life was tragically cut short in an airplane crash in 1967, just as his career had hit its stride.

The Queen of Soul is Detroit-born Aretha Franklin. Like so many other black singers, Aretha was raised in the church-music tradition; her father was a Baptist minister, and she and her brothers and sisters sang in the choir. By the time she was eighteen, she was a veteran soloist with an itch to make her mark as a blues singer.

Her moment finally came when she began recording for Atlantic Records, a company with a long experience in producing black performers. Few singers ever become instant, overnight permanent stars; Aretha did. Gifted with a remarkable vocal range and an instinct for presenting a song, Aretha Franklin has held a consistently strong position in rhythm-and-blues popularity polls for years.

In the early sixties, small, local record companies sometimes blossomed into national labels, often on the strength of a few performers in a particular type of music. One such company was Stax Records, named after its two founders, Jim Stewart and Estelle Axton. Stax worked out a deal with Atlantic Records to market its products nationwide, and then began releasing songs by local performers. By 1962, the new company had several top-sellers to its credit, and had acquired a house band called Booker T and the MG's.

Booker T had Jones for a last name, and played keyboards in the group. The MG's (which stood for Memphis Group) were guitarist Steve Cropper, bassist Donald "Duck" Dunn, and drummer Al Jackson. The group was something of a novelty in rock, being racially integrated (two black, two white), and their style was about equal parts gospel and country. Furthermore, they set the tone for Stax recordings throughout the sixties.

Stax scored successes with a number of other performers from around the country: Sam (Moore) and Dave (Prater) from Miami; the Staples Singers, a family act that moved from gospel to R & B, from Chicago; Carla Thomas, who had majored in English at a Nashville college; Otis Redding from Georgia; and bald superstar Isaac Hayes from nearby Covington, Tennessee. Hays began with Stax as a keyboard player, but proved to have great talent for writing songs.

Hayes rocketed to prominence by turning out lush arrangements for large instrumental groups, notably on an album called *Hot Buttered Soul* in 1969. The experience led to the film score for the motion picture *Shaft*, followed by two other film tracks and a binful of other albums (*The Isaac Hayes Movement, Black Moses, Chocolate Chip*, and so on). For all his success and talent, however, Hayes ended his career in bankruptcy.

At the other pole of soul, perhaps, is the lovely lyric singing and keyboard playing of Roberta Flack. Born in Asheville, North Carolina, Roberta grew up in a musical family and majored in music and education at college. After a stint as a school teacher, she broke in as a vocalist and soon became a fixture in the Atlantic Records lineup of singers. Her smooth, well-controlled voice combines the best of traditional schooling with black phrasing and rhythm.

Even as Memphis and Stax Records were extending America's musical geography, a true phenomenon was emerging to the north, in the Motor Capital of the World, Detroit. In the 1950s, Berry Gordy owned a record store specializing in jazz records. Fortunately, it went bankrupt. Fortunately? Well, you see, he switched to writing rhythm-and-blues songs, and later to producing them himself. It was a tough scuffle for several years, but Gordy stayed with it, and eventually created Tamla Records, his own label.

His first great national success came with his discovery of a Detroit quintet called the Miracles and their songwriter and lead singer, Bill Smokey Robinson. Operating from a modest white house on Detroit's West Grand Boulevard, Tamla Records soon burgeoned into the nation's largest, most successful business that was entirely owned and operated by black entrepreneurs.

Although both Gordy and Robinson were talented songwriters themselves, Tamla and its sister labels (VIP, Rare Earth, Motown, Soul, Gordy) really soared after "HDH" joined the company. "HDH" were Lamont Dozier and the dapper Holland brothers, Brian and Eddie. These three, working from the ideas of Gordy and Robinson, created the classic Motown Sound that characterized the Detroit groups and that scored hit after nationwide hit.

The Motown Sound features tight, disciplined rhythms, gospel-flavored harmonies, smooth singers who seldom resort to shouty or growly vocal sounds, and songs with refrains that recycle the song's feature line of text (for example, "Ain't No Mountain High Enough") again and again. When performing live, the Motown groups often liven their songs with choreography as well-machined as a Cadillac V-8, giving visual comment and added excitement to the music. Through the 1960s and into the early 1970s, the Motown Sound was the sound of success. The formula finally wore thin, as such formulas do, but it left a legacy of fine performances that is a standard for the future.

The name "Motown" is a contraction of Detroit's nickname, the Motor City. It was appropriate in many ways, for not only was Berry Gordy a Detroiter, but so were many of his performers—Smokey Robinson and the Miracles, Diana Ross and the Supremes, Stevie Wonder (actually from nearby Saginaw), and the Four Tops. Other acts the company picked up from various places—Marvin Gaye from his native Washington, DC; Gladys Knight and the Pips from their hometown, Atlanta; the Isley Brothers from Cincinnati; and the Jackson Five, featuring Michael Jackson, from Gary, Indiana.

If Berry Gordy made a mistake, it was probably that he stuck with a good thing for too long. When the Motown productions began to falter, there were others eager to take up the slack. Not least of these was the studio of Philadelphia International Records, run by Ken Gamble and Leon Huff. The style of Philly International's Sigma Sound Studios was a slick reworking of the Motown formula, featuring string-section backgrounds and a more prominent drum sound. Wilson Pickett and the O'jays (named for a deejay who had plugged the group) were among the top Philadelphia performers. When disco music became the national craze early in the 1970s, Philly

International was ready with "TSOP" (The Sound of Philadelphia), perhaps the company's best-known single.

Meanwhile, on the West Coast, a young, black disc jockey named Sylvester Stewart put together a remarkable group called Sly and the Family Stone. Blending soul and disco with occasional overtones of chaos, the racially integrated group rose with meteoric speed, and fell just as fast when Sly would suddenly decide not to show up for a job. His vocal style returned to a sound the Detroit and Philadelphia groups had nearly abandoned—the gospelly, gravelly, shouty soul sound of black folk music. Folks called it funk, borrowing a term that had already been applied to jazz.

Other groups soon picked up on funk in one or another of its many forms. One vocal group assumed a schizophrenic double identity, recording for one company as the Parliaments and for another label as Funkadelic. The Chicago-based group Earth, Wind, and Fire, with its tight ensembles, stabbing horn figures, and extravagant light-and-movement production, is another exponent of modern funk.

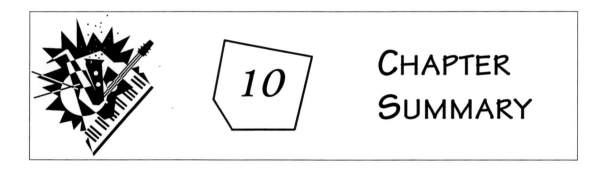

CHAPTER SUMMARY

The 1960s and 1970s were prosperous times for a number of black pop-rock groups and businessmen. Some continued in the tradition of gospel and blues singing, the rough vocals and frank lyrics that were called soul. Others blended black musical styles with white country, or with the smooth, well-drilled precision of the studio bands to create the enormously successful Motown Sound. The distinctions between white and black popular music became finer and finer as black groups gained a widening audience during the seventies.

Suggested Projects

1. Compare recordings of Aretha Franklin and Roberta Flack. What differences do you notice? What similarities? Write a report on your observations. Other comparisons you may wish to make: Sly and the Family Stone with the Temptations; Booker T and the MGs with Earth, Wind, and Fire.

2. Stevie Wonder's first album was entitled *Little Stevie Wonder the 12-Year-Old Genius.* What other child prodigies in music can you find? How were their lives like, or different from, Stevie's? Write a three- or four-page report on your findings.

3. Give an oral report illustrated with recorded examples on one of the performers or groups discussed in this chapter.

Suggested Records

There are too many groups listed in this chapter for any list of recordings to encompass. Recordings of any of the artists mentioned may be used to illustrate their style.

11 ART ROCK— OR IS IT?

One can make some interesting comparisons between rock and so-called art, or classical, music—Bach, Mozart, Beethoven, and such. Let's consider a few comparisons. Rock is highly theatrical; so is opera. Rock uses high volume levels; so do Mahler symphonies and Strauss tone poems. Rock has sections to display the performing skills of the musicians; that's what solo concertos are all about.

Not surprising, then, that the fast-evolving music of rock and the many styles of art music should begin to draw together. In fact, as a generation of young musicians grew up hearing both rock and the classics all their lives, it was probably inevitable that the two streams of musical thought should merge from time to time. Such a coming together of art and jazz music created a new sound called "third stream music." The blending of classics and rock, still in its early stages, is often called art rock.

This new kind of music takes ideas and effects from both the Western and certain Eastern classical-music traditions. Sometimes art-rock musicians simply parody well-known compositions, as in the Emerson, Lake, and Palmer version of Mussorgsky's *Pictures at an Exhibition* or Tomita's translation of Holst's *Planets* for the synthesizer. Occasionally the rock musicians will use forms borrowed from the classical music of Europe—the song cycle, as in Stevie Wonder's *Journey into the Secret Life of Plants*, or the opera, such as the Who's *Tommy*. Some groups use effects such as exotic scales or odd-number meters or rhythm cycles, ideas that are common in Islamic or Hindu musical systems.

Beginnings

The first widely publicized gestures toward art rock were taken by those seminal innovators, the Beatles. The 1967 album called *Sergeant Pepper's Lonely Hearts Club Band* used an orchestra and a hundred-voice choir—musical forces that one usually associates with the operas of Richard Wagner. Somewhat earlier they had added the majestic Indian *sitar* to their collection of electrically amplified guitars. While the *sitar* was used more as an exotic guitar than as an Indian classical instrument, it still brought to the attention of an international audience the world of Indian classical music.

Other personalities and groups soon flocked toward the new paths the Beatles had marked. Even the Rolling Stones used a *sitar* from time to time. The Moody Blues' album *Every Good Boy Deserves Favour* incorporates a soft-rock group as a sort of *concertino* group against a lush, mellow symphony orchestra. Keith Emerson, who was working with a group called The Nice, recorded his galloping rendition of themes from Dvorák's *New World Symphony* (and Bernstein's "America" from *West Side Story*) on a 1967 album.

After Keith Emerson left The Nice, he joined forces with guitarist Greg Lake and drummer Carl Palmer. Emerson, whose onstage cavorting was exceeded only by his formidable skill as an organist, led the group through a number of recordings featuring arrangements of standard classics. The previously mentioned *Pictures at an Exhibition* album was one of these; others include a romping, rocking version of Aaron Copland's "Hoedown" from the ballet score *Rodeo*.

English Art Rock

By 1970, the synthesis of rock with various art-music styles was well under way, especially in England. One group that illustrates this blending was called Gentle Giant. Three of the band's original members were brothers—bassist Ray, xylophonist Phil, and singer Derek Schulman. Their father was a professional jazz musician in England, and much of his feeling for jazz shows up in his sons' work. They introduced the English madrigal style and complex meters. Some of GG's work is wonderfully lighthearted and witty, such as "School Days" from the album *Three Friends*. Other songs, however, are scaldingly bitter about life and human nature—for instance, "Peel the Paint," from the same album, has the same theme as the novel *Lord of the Flies*. Like folk rock, this was music to be *listened* to, rather than *danced* to.

One of the most successful of the art-rock bands commercially is Genesis. Formed originally by three school chums headed by Peter Gabriel, the group has experienced some remarkable ups and downs. In 1975, leader Gabriel suddenly left the group, and most fans thought that Genesis could not survive. Instead, drummer Phil Collins stepped forward, and the band proceeded to cut one of its finest albums, *Trick of the Tail*. This album comes close to being a collection of twentieth-century art songs, from the sweet but slightly loony "Mad Man Moon" to the catchy and comic title song. While Genesis is uneven in the quality of their product, with a perennial eye on the pop charts, they can be extraordinarily musical, as this album shows. In the 1980s, Genesis changed style to a group with more popular appeal.

One of the most innovative and successful of the art-rock groups is Yes. Like most rock groups, the personnel of Yes has changed from time to time, but usually the nucleus has been singer Jon Anderson, guitarist Steve Howe, and bass player Chris Squire. The group first took its inspiration from Emerson, Lake, and Palmer (ELP), thus earning the sneering classification of techno-rock (that is, all technique and no feeling) from some rock critics. Yes quickly evolved, however, into a group that explored larger forms and concept albums with remarkable musicality and control of their material.

Exploring unusual meters, sound effects, and rhythm cycles is a Yes specialty. Listen, for example, to "South Side of the Sky," from Yes's *Fragile* album. The piece begins with the sound of wind blowing, as if across a broad, frozen field. Then bass and guitar break into a repeating riff that accompanies Anderson's singing ("A river, a mountain . . ."). After three verses of this rather dense polyphony, the pattern breaks, and a syncopated piano figure in a seven-beat meter appears. This ends with a cymbal splash and more wind noises. After a cadenza, the piano picks up a new figure in a ten-beat meter. Soon we hear a three-voice choral section ("La, la, la . . .") with the rhythm section. Another piano break, back to the "la-las," and the section closes with piano and wind. Suddenly, the music at the beginning returns, and the piece fades out with instrumental solos.

What is noteworthy here is the concern for structure, for contrast, for symmetry and unity. The wind sound is used as a common theme to stitch the piece together. The piano becomes the main character of the middle section, though it plays different things in different parts. Jon Anderson's symbolist lyrics seem to be about climbing a high mountain, which gives relevance to the wind sounds. However, the words might just as well be about struggling with life, using the mountain as a metaphor. Clearly, though, this is not the average pop song. The structure, the strange meters, the propulsive rhythms, the concern for contrast are all parts of Yes's style.

An even more ambitious work is the mini-symphony, "Close to the Edge," from the album of the same name. This major work (it takes one whole side of the record) is a masterpiece of art-rock devices. It is divided into four sections, without pauses between. Each section has its own text, and three of the sections (one, two, and four) share most of the thematic ideas. The third section is slow, and has very different themes from the rest. This work is described and analyzed in the Listening Guide at the end of this chapter.

The improvisation-oriented group King Crimson, led by guitarist Robert Fripp, was one of the most radically different groups in art rock. The only common denominator to the various King Crimson albums is Fripp himself, other personnel having floated around with extraordinary frequency. However, the group at one time or another included Greg Lake, of ELP, and Bill Bruford, Yes's wizard drummer. Some of King Crimson's best music seems strange, even alien, to a dedicated rock fan. Fripp has always had close ties with avant-garde jazz, and much of the group's best work— *Lizard, Larks' Tongues in Aspic,* or *Starless and Bible Black*—more closely resembles the music of Herbie Hancock or Miles Davis than it does that of Fats Domino or Elvis Costello. In the last analysis, Fripp resembles only Robert Fripp. He blazed new trails that defy categorization.

To get the flavor of King Crimson at their far-out best, listen to "Larks' Tongues in Aspic, Part I" from the album with the same name. The piece begins with a long section for African *sansa*, or thumb piano. Jingling bells gradually swell and replace the *sansa*. There follows a series of episodes that seem to have no connection, at times heavy rock, at times a rhythmic ostinato by the violin. The section ends in a Bartókian soliloquy for solo violin, then a faintly Oriental-sounding duet for violin and a dulcimer-type instrument. The section ends (it's hard to tell, because the record is not banded) with a somber melody on electric bass, with violin counterpoint, and with unintelligible voices in the background.

Another rock guitarist who explored unconventional territory was John McLaughlin. He began as a jazz guitarist, and was brilliant enough to record two albums with premier jazz trumpeter Miles Davis. McLaughlin's strong philosophical bent drew him to Hindu mysticism, and led him to form the Mahavishnu Orchestra, a rock ensemble that blended authentic Indian music with Western rock.

The Mahavishnu Orchestra went through a series of incarnations before disappearing completely. The recordings they made were sometimes pompous, sometimes lovely and expressive. For a brief spell, French violinist Jean-Luc Ponty was with the group. It took competent musicians to follow the complex rhythm cycles and modal scales of classical Hindu music. Listen, for example, to "Wings of Karma," from the album *Apocalypse*. After a free-flowing introduction by the orchestra, the rock band takes up a steady riff:

accompanied by a jazz beat from the drums. This riff, in an eleven-beat meter, backs up an improvisory solo by McLaughlin. Later on, Ponty solos, with the orchestra accompanying him, but now the riff has stretched to a twenty-one-beat cycle. The entire piece rounds out nicely into an ABA design with a concluding slow section.

The rock band Jethro Tull, featuring Ian Anderson, the prancing flutist, adopts Anglo-Irish folk music as its signature, well mixed with an occasional odd-meter piece and a generally heavy rock beat. Scottish-born Anderson is the single constant element in the band's history of revolving personnel. The folk music influence can readily be heard in the tricky "Pine Marten's Jig" from the album *A*. For another side to Tull, listen to "Batteries Not Included" on the same album, an acid comment on the mechanization of people in a high-tech society.

Art Rock Outside England

While most of the significant contributions of art rock originated in England, there were many non-English groups that pioneered in the idiom. One was the French group called Gong, whose most constant members were Didier Malherbe and Pierre

Moerlen. Gong produced some interesting records, sometimes revealing influences from Indonesian *gamelan* music. A second French group, called Magma, creates complex but sometimes pompous music that, according to drummer-leader Christian van Zander, draws inspiration from Igor Stravinsky and Karlheinz Stockhausen.

Italy's contribution to art rock rests on the work of a group called Premiata Forneria Marconi, usually known as PFM for short. The group has been strongly influenced by both King Crimson and Emerson, Lake, and Palmer. A fine, tight ensemble, PFM recorded some memorable cuts, including "Four Holes in the Ground," from the album *The World Becomes the World*, a rollicking, lyrical tarantella in five-eighths time; or the title song, a dark but moving canticle.

On this side of the Atlantic, art rock got off to a rather slow start. Perhaps the first group here to begin using art-rock effects systematically was Kansas, a six-member group based in Topeka. Basically a popular-music group, Kansas makes occasional use of odd meters and has a few numbers that qualify as art rock. For example, listen to the song "Magnum Opus," from the album *Two for the Show*. This piece illustrates some of the art-music effects that have also been used by other groups mentioned.

Another American group with roots in art music is the Dregs, an unpredictable assemblage that began as the Dixie Dregs at the School of Music of the University of Miami. Recordings of the Dregs are dizzying collections of widely varying styles of music; one piece sounds like something written by French composer Erik Satie ("Old World," from the album *Dregs of the Earth*), while another is a sassy rhythm-and-blues number ("Broadway Strut," from the same album) and a third is a rompin', stompin', country breakdown *à la* Charlie Daniels ("Pride o' the Farm," same album). Listen to their tunes, and you may discover that the meter is fifteen, or there is an atonal chord progression, or perhaps a segment that is purely electronic music. The Dregs are both virtuosic and versatile, and command a remarkably broad range of styles.

Other Groups with Art-Rock Influences

The groups described above are among the leaders in the art-rock movement, but are by no means the only groups involved. Many of the following groups contain members, or ex-members, of groups already mentioned. The band called UK, for example, originally included John Wetton from King Crimson on bass, Bill Bruford from both Yes and King Crimson on drums, and Alan Holdsworth of Gong on guitar, as well as Eddie Jobson on keyboards. Similarly, Asia comprises John Wetton again, Carl Palmer of ELP as drummer, and Steve Howe (guitar) and Geoff Downs (keyboards) from Yes. Other bands of note are the American groups Crack the Sky and Zebra. Even basically pop groups like Toto or new-wave bands such as The Police use art-rock effects.

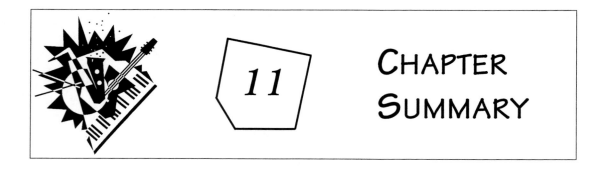

CHAPTER SUMMARY

11

Since about 1970, a number of rock bands have incorporated characteristics of Western and non-Western art music as part of their style. The art-rock movement has been strongest in England, but is increasingly evident in other nations, including the United States. Each band approaches the synthesis in its own way, but among the effects used are odd meters and rhythm cycles, quoting from standard works of art music, electronic composition, the use of formal structures typical of art music, and the exploitation of exotic scales borrowed from other cultures.

Suggested Projects

1. Compare the Emerson, Lake, and Palmer version of *Pictures at an Exhibition* with an orchestral version of the same piece. What differences do you notice? Why do you think ELP chose the sections they did of the original work to interpret? Write a three- or four-page paper answering these questions.

2. The title of this chapter suggests two questions: "Is it art music?"; and "Is it rock?" What do you think? Write a two- or three-page essay on why you believe as you do.

3. It might be interesting to follow one of the groups through several recordings, seeing how the personnel change. Or perhaps you would like to follow some of the performers through several groups. Write a two-page report on one of these topics. Yes and King Crimson are two groups whose members you might find interesting to trace. Feel free to pick from among other groups if you wish.

Suggested Records

Recordings of any of the groups mentioned may be used to illustrate the various characteristics. Since all groups keep a sharp eye on the popular-music market, they all have pop-style tunes on record. The following recordings have been referred to in the preceding text, and constitute a beginning collection for the study of art rock.

Blood, Sweat and Tears. *Blood, Sweat and Tears.* Columbia PC 9720.

Dixie Dregs. *Dregs of the Earth.* Arista AL 9528.

Genesis. *Trick of the Tail.* Atco SD 38-101.

Gentle Giant. *Three Friends.* Columbia 31649.

Jethro Tull. *A.* Chrysalis CHE 1301.

Kansas. *Two for the Show.* Kirshner 35660.

King Crimson. *Larks' Tongues in Aspic.* Atlantic SD 7263.

Mahavishnu Orchestra. *Apocalypse.* Columbia C32957.

Moody Blues. *Every Good Boy Deserves Favour.* Threshold THS 5.

PFM. *The World Became the World.* Manticore MC 66673.

Yes. *Close to the Edge.* Atlantic SD 7244.

Yes. *Fragile.* Atlantic SD 19132.

LISTENING GUIDE: Description and Analysis of "Close to the Edge," by Yes.

"Close to the Edge" is divided into four sections without pauses between them. The sections are subtitled, "The Solid Time of Change," "Total Mass Retain," "I Get Up, I Get Down," and "Seasons of Man." The first section begins with the sound of running water and birdcalls. Gradually, a chord emerges from this background, swells, and finally erupts in a heavy rock jamming with ascending scales in the bass. A single vocal chord interrupts the jamming, but the instruments immediately return. Again a vocal chord, again the instruments. A third chord marks the transition to the first important theme, played first by the guitar. This breaks off at an organ chord, the meter shifts, and Anderson sings the second theme. The first section ends just as Anderson sings the final words printed on the record sleeve.

The second section begins with a wonderful cross-meter effect. The bass plays a heavy riff in 4/4 meter:

This part repeats while Anderson sings the second melody from Section I in 6/8 meter:

However, the two figures do not coincide at the bar lines; rather, they both have the same eighth-note length, which makes the 6/8 measures only three-quarters as long as the 4/4 measures:

The effect is brilliant, a musical magician's trick of seeming to do two totally unrelated things at once and yet having it all work out at the end.

This effect breaks off into the second theme from Section I, which in turn leads to another polymetric section based on a new bass riff:

The new riff accompanies the first theme from Section I.

The tempo suddenly dies, and we are in the third section. Random sounds, hinting at previous melodies, can be heard. Gradually, a steady beat marked by synthesizer chords emerges. A choral section leads to Anderson's solo, using a new melody, and with choral comments on Anderson's part. A gradual crescendo leads to a passage of massive organ chords. There is a brief reprise of the "I get up, I get down" theme, more organ chords, and the section ends as the synthesizer plays a brilliant flourish.

The final section plunges violently into the first theme again, played by the whole band. There is a jam section on the second theme, then Anderson sings the second theme, while the bass plays a variant of the cross-meter effect, this time in 3/4 meter. Suddenly, everyone is all together on a closing passage, based on the first "I get up, I get down" melody. The piece fades back into the sounds of birds and running water.

12 JAZZ-ROCK AND FUSION

In Chapter 2 we sketched the development of popular music up to 1950. The improvised music called jazz, which had provided the energy and the excitement for the music of the swing bands, mutated in several directions in the 1950s, becoming music for listening rather than for dancing. Two broad styles of jazz emerged: *bop*, based on the music of trumpeter Dizzy Gillespie, saxophonist Charlie Parker, pianist Thelonious Monk, and others; and *cool jazz*, developed by trumpeter Miles Davis, saxophonist Stan Getz, pianist/arranger Gil Evans, and others. Bop and cool became contrasting styles of jazz, the one employing fast improvisation with the emphasis on display of technique, the other stressing clever, lush arrangements and thoughtful and expressive solos. Any given group of the period was mostly associated with one of these styles, but all groups played in both styles from time to time.

A curious relationship sprang up between early rock and 1950s jazz. Rock 'n' rollers took over many of the terms and images used by the jazzmen, but utterly changed, even reversed, their meanings. "Cool" jazz was a subtle, mellow, blending style; in rock, "cool" meant noisy, strident, aggressive. The "big bopper" of rock 'n' roll myth played a music light-years removed from the edgy, technically demanding music of jazz's big boppers, Gillespie and Parker. Even the exotic uniform adopted by jazz enthusiasts and created by Thelonious Monk—beret, goatee, sunglasses worn indoors—became the rocker's model, though jazz was played mostly in clubs, while rock 'n' roll was largely a dance-hall phenomenon.

Just as rock spun off new and often competing styles and performers, so did jazz. In the 1960s, *funky jazz*, blues-flavored and swinging, emerged, as epitomized by the Horace Silver ensembles. So did dissonant, driving *hard-bop regression* movement led by saxophonist Sonny Rollins and trumpeter Clifford Brown, and the bizarre experiments in *free jazz* pioneered by trumpeter Don Cherry and saxophonist Ornette Coleman. Meanwhile, jazz had moved into concert halls, as well as nightclubs and summer festivals, especially in Europe. The Modern Jazz Quartet pushed their intellectual chamber jazz to new triumphs. The Dave Brubeck Quartet and British pianist George

Shearing, among many others, became regular fixtures on the concert circuit. Maynard Ferguson, Stan Kenton, and Buddy Rich kept big-band jazz very much alive.

The day inevitably arrived when the musically sophisticated in both jazz and rock discovered one another. Highly trained musicians, raised on rock but entranced with the musical range and subtlety of jazz, welded the two styles into a genre called (reasonably enough) *jazz-rock*. In the late 1960s, the groups called Blood, Sweat and Tears and Chicago Transit Authority (later shortened to just Chicago) turned out a series of successful albums in the new style, combining a heavy rock beat with tight arrangements for winds and including jazz–style jamming in solos. Blood, Sweat and Tears had as its core a group of students at the Eastman Rochester School of Music, and presented occasional arrangements by band members Dick Halligan and Fred Lipsius of works by Prokofiev or Satie. Chicago modeled their sound on black hard–bop bands and vocals.

Soon cool-jazz founder Miles Davis, whose various groups served as the finishing school for cutting-edge jazz performers for forty years, struck a blow for jazz-rock with an album called *Bitches Brew*. The name for the new style of music became *jazz-rock fusion*, or simply *fusion*. Like solar fusion, the process soon produced new elements with interesting possibilities. British guitarist John McLaughlin, a Miles Davis sideman on the *Brew* album, joined with drummer Billy Cobham as the nucleus of the Mahavishnu Orchestra (see Chapter 11). Still later, McLaughlin, a formidable guitarist, became so involved in Indian music and philosophy that he formed an acoustic trio, called Shakti, with an Indian violinist and a drummer.

More graduates of Davis groups explored the possibilities of fusion with often fascinating results. Austrian pianist Joe Zawinul, once part of jazz saxophonist Cannonball Adderly's group, joined with tenor sax player Wayne Shorter and formed Weather Report, a long-lived ensemble with many recordings to its credit. Ex-Davis pianist Chick Corea organized a musically adventurous ensemble, Return to Forever, with Stanley Clarke on bass, Lenny White on drums, and Al diMeola on guitar. These four talented and awesomely competent performers meshed well, turning out true ensemble music rather than a series of virtuosic solos. The basic sound owes much to art-rock groups such as Yes or King Crimson, with prominent ostinatos, riffs with meters like 10 or 7, and unisonal sections played with astonishing technique. They also varied the texture and volume often, creating a sort of chamber music enlivened by some solid funk. No listing of fusion groups can fail to mention keyboardist Herbie Hancock, yet another Davis veteran, who played a number of keyboard instruments, including synthesizers, as the core of a number of successful groups.

On the pop side of the jazz-rock spectrum, the commercially very successful group Spyro Gyra launched album after album of cleverly written, well-performed music which might be called Fusion Lite. The six-member ensemble welds Caribbean rhythms to an Earth, Wind, and Fire-style horn line of trumpet, trombone, and alto saxophone. Spyro Gyra's trademark sound—stabbing horn syncopations over a loping beat, played with cheerful verve—is a danceable crowd-pleaser. The work of this group and of Return to Forever may be taken as representing the polar extremes of the jazz-rock continuum.

Like bop or cool jazz, fusion has become another style of music that various groups may use for certain pieces. Besides becoming an interesting style of its own, it enriches both mainstream jazz and rock music with its broadened possibilities.

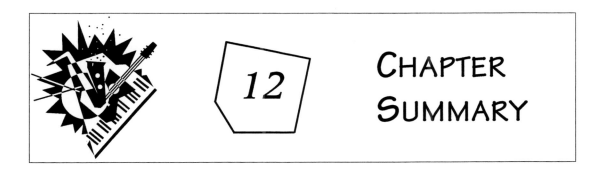

12 CHAPTER SUMMARY

Jazz evolved alongside rock for nearly twenty years before the two idioms joined hands in the work of particular groups, notably Blood, Sweat and Tears and Chicago. Trumpet player Miles Davis and many of the veterans of his various groups advanced the course of fusion in many experimental performances and recordings. The group Weather Report, based on pianist Joe Zawinul and saxophonist Wayne Shorter, was the longest-running fusion group and made numerous albums. Herbie Hancock and Chick Corea made some of the most notable advances in fusion. Meanwhile, jazz-rock found a solid commercial niche in the work of New York-based Spyro Gyra.

Suggested Projects

1. Many words are shared by both jazz and rock fans, but they often have different meanings. Give an oral report to the class on how the terms *cool*, *bop*, *funky*, and *swing* differ in their jazz and rock contexts. Try to discover the original meaning of the terms, as applied to music.

2. Compare a jazz-rock recording with one of, say, 1950s rock 'n' roll or a Beatles performance or a Jan and Dean/Beach Boys production. What differences do you notice? What similarities do you hear? Write a report on your comparisons.

3. Miles Davis was influential in the development of both mainstream jazz and fusion. Research and report on his life, summarizing your findings for the class.

Suggested Records

Dozens of recordings by the performers mentioned above are available, most of which illustrate well the jazz-rock idiom. The following are representative selections.

Blood, Sweat and Tears. *Blood, Sweat and Tears.* Columbia PC 9720.

Chicago. *Chicago Transit Authority.* Columbia GQ 33255 PG8.

Davis, Miles. *Bitches Brew.* Columbia G2K 40577; CD.

Hancock, Herbie. *Sound-System.* Columbia FC 39478.

Return to Forever. *Romantic Warrior.* CBS PC 34076.

Spyro Gyra. *Carnaval.* MCA 5149.

Weather Report. *This Is This.* Columbia CK 40280; CD.

LISTENING GUIDE 1: "Majestic Dance," by Return to Forever. From *Romantic Warrior,* CBS PC 34076.

The work opens with a guitar playing a rhythmic figure, soon joined by the rest of the quartet and set to a solid rock beat. There are short solos by the keyboards and the guitar from time to time, interwoven with quick unisonal figures by all the members or dialog sections between keyboard and the guitar/bass combination. The drumming is far more than just time–keeping, with intricate cross-rhythms complementing what the other instruments are doing. This is plainly ensemble music, with no protracted solos for any instrument. The piece ends on a low drone from bass and synthesizer.

LISTENING GUIDE 2: "Cashaça," by Spyro Gyra. From *Carnaval,* MCA 5149.

The keyboards begin a riff, which is soon joined by several Latin American instruments. The piano plays a short idea, answered by the horns over a steady rhythm. A saxophone improvises a solo over the Latin rhythm, with brass punctuations. A synthesizer takes a solo while the horns and rhythm play riffs. The opening idea in the horns recurs, followed by the first piano-and-Latin figure. The horns play a slow scalar passage upward. A guitar solos, punctuated by syncopations in the horns. This fades out at the end. This is much closer to the traditional structure of ensemble-solo-solo-solo-ensemble of both jazz and rock performances than the previous piece.

13 DISCO, REGGAE, PUNK, NEW WAVE, AND WHATEVER

The eruption of rock styles that took place in the 1960s led to even more, and more extreme, kinds of rock in the 1970s. Some of these new styles were spin-offs of some of the 1960s innovations. Others were attempts to get back to the original social function of rock—to shock, to outrage, to bug the squares. At root, however, the fact was that rock, as a popular idiom, was running out of steam, groping ever more desperately for the means to keep going. Whenever you see a musical style recycling its original material in revivals, you know that the style is having trouble staying creative.

Disco

Disco music is a case in point. Disco is body music, just as the music of Fats Domino and Chubby Checker is body music. It was to be danced to, not seriously listened to, and it had no more purpose than that. Name all the great disco bands you can think of. Chances are, you can't think of any. There is no Simon and Garfunkel, no Joni Mitchell, in disco. You're supposed to dance, not think about the song.

Disco's style is homogeneous, even homogenized. Performers aren't important. The music itself typically has a relentless beat, impelled by the whop, whop of a pile-driving bass drum. The tempo stays the same from song to song. There may be intricate layers of rhythm, borrowing from African and Jamaican reggae music. The melody is usually a slick and soulless arrangement of a tune you already know—pop songs, other rock tunes, even (sacrilege!) classics by Beethoven, Mozart, or someone else. Lots of violins, some bluesy wailing by a vocal group, and there you have it—instant disco.

This disco craze began in New York in the early 1970s, and spread across the country, mostly in nightclubs in large cities. The term "disco" is a contraction of "discotheque," meaning a French dance hall where the music is provided from recordings, rather than by a live band. Disco exploded on the American consciousness after the release of the film *Saturday Night Fever*, starring John Travolta. For a year or so, it seemed that disco music burbled from every radio, every "boom box," every automobile in the nation. The fever passed almost as quickly as it came on, however. While some people still visit discotheques, the fad has run its course, and you seldom hear disco on a popular-music station today.

Reggae

The sun-soaked Caribbean island of Jamaica is a long way from the sound studios of Philadelphia or London. It may seem strange that the music of this tropical land should influence popular music in this country. Still, the music of the Caribbean has had a strong impact on American pop music in the past—most recently in the Cuban *mambo* craze of the 1950s and Harry Belafonte's calypso songs—so the new sound of reggae had a rather familiar ring when it began showing up in current pop records.

No one knows just where the word "reggae" (pronounced RAY-gay) came from. Whatever its origin, it has a distinctive sound. Most of the effects are rhythmic. Accents are placed on beats two and four in a four-beat measure. The acoustic guitar plays a steady "chinga-chinga" pattern. Sometimes horns are used in reggae; some of the pieces of Earth, Wind, and Fire show a lot of reggae influence. The sound of reggae came to Britain through the large communities of Jamaicans living there. Probably the best-known Jamaican reggae band was Bob Marley and the Wailers. The words to their songs are often full of the symbolism of their Rastafarian religion, and are meaningless to others. Marley died of brain and lung cancer on May 11, 1981. You can hear reggae influences in the music of many new-wave groups, such as The Police.

Punk Rock

Girls with bright orange mohawk haircuts and scarlet lipstick. Boys with black-dyed hair in cocklebur spikes and large safety pins inserted through their cheeks. Leather jackets over T-shirts, leather-look thigh-high boots and miniskirts. Central Casting characters for *A Clockwork Orange*? No, punk rockers.

Punk rock is not just aggressive, not just antisocial. Punk rock is nihilistic. Punkers are against everything. Punk emerged from the pubs of London as an expression of the frustration and anger of the long-unemployed workers and of kids raised in hopeless slums. In their crude language and cruder behavior, punkers gave expression to the feelings of fed-up blue-collar Britishers.

The model for punk bands was established by the Sex Pistols. The group was created in 1975 by Malcolm McLaren, owner of an exclusive London clothes shop called, incongruously, Sex. In his off-duty time, Malcolm acted as manager for various rock bands. He picked up three out-of-work instrumentalists and added a strutting, sneering lead singer (who had never sung) named John Lydon, alias Johnny Rotten.

As a musical unit, the Sex Pistols were raw and amateurish. To their fans, musical deficiencies were more than made up for by their undisguised hostility. A recording contract with Britain's EMI led to their first single, "Anarchy in the U.K.," but the arrangement with the band immediately soured. EMI was acutely embarrassed by the band's obscene language on a TV interview. The recording executives squirmed, but the publicity sent the Sex Pistols' fame soaring. Other similar incidents finally led EMI to cancel their contract. Their next contract, with A & M Records, lasted exactly a week, and was canceled for unacceptable conduct. No club in Britain would book them, no record company would market them—so they fired their bass player and added Johnny Rotten's friend, Sid Vicious, in his place.

A new recording contract, with the ironically named Virgin Records, led to a series of singles and an album before the band fell apart in 1978. Sid Vicious lived up to his name, murdering his girlfriend a year later. Johnny Rotten ducked into a telephone booth, and came out mild-mannered John Lydon, proclaiming the futility of punk and the death of rock 'n' roll.

The Sex Pistols were through, but they left behind a legacy of raunchy music and a veritable army of imitators. The most successful of the imitators was The Clash, a shrewder and less self-destructive group than their forerunners. Beginning as a punk band, The Clash has gradually moved in the direction of new wave, one ear tuned to outrage, the other to the ring of the cash register. The Clash hoped to be the focus of punk's anti-culture; but instead of leading the punk revolution, they have ended up in the role of followers of punk fashion. Revolutions have always had a way of swallowing their own children.

Heavy Metal and Glitz Rock

The textbook definition of a heavy metal is one of the metallic elements, like uranium or plutonium, which appear near the end of the Periodic Table of Elements. In music, the term describes wall-shaking, ear-numbing, distorted, hyper-amplified aggression. The logical extension of the acid-rock and Jimi Hendrix developments, heavy metal bands carry both guitar technique and feedback distortion to new extremes.

The prototype heavy-metal band is Led Zeppelin (1968–80), a British band that was founded, led, and produced by guitarist Jimmy Page. The Zep, as its fans have nicknamed the group, evolved a thunderous, screaming sound expanded and diffused by reverb and leaning heavily on bass and drums for its power. These qualities became the stock-in-trade of heavy metal bands everywhere.

With this for a beginning (1968), other heavy metal bands sprang up from the gentle soil of England like amanita mushrooms. Groups formed, fell apart, then reformed with dizzying frequency, often with virtually the same members. Thus Deep Purple first appeared in 1968 changing personnel every few years, and in 1978 color-shifted into a succession of Whitesnakes. Similarly, Black Sabbath (1969) hived off

Ozzie Osbourne and later shared vocalists with Rainbow, which in turn contributed some members to a new Deep Purple incarnation. Other British groups in the genre include Judas Priest (formed 1973), Motörhead (1975), Iron Maiden (1977), and Def Leppard (1978).

Foreign imitators emerged in the 1970s. The durable group AC/DC formed in Australia in 1974 and found success in Britain and the United States. America produced a spate of groups, including Aerosmith, Motley Crüe, and Blue Öyster Cult (umlauted letters seem to be an American penchant), and wiz guitarist Eddie van Halen. Petite, red-haired Pat Benatar trained to sing opera, but opted for the glamour and money of rock instead. And Metallica sprang from Los Angeles in 1983 and found a niche with passionate speed-metal freaks.

Musically, heavy metal employs mind-numbing volume, repeating riffs, and power chords from the guitars. One variant, speed metal, includes guitar solos played as fast as possible over a jackhammer beat from the drums. The music inspires devotees to engage in head-banging (against a wall or with each other) and "moshing," or launching oneself as a projectile at other dancers, heedless of possible damage.

Other bands adopted the heavy-metal sound and image. Among noteworthy British groups, we should mention Deep Purple, Bad Company, and Ozzie Osbourne's group Black Sabbath, with its reputation for having satanic-cult connections.

The bizarre and grotesque aspects of rock reached new extremes in a number of groups that traded musical prowess for theatricality. Ultimate honors in the class of glitz rock, perhaps, should be shared by the weirdly painted ensemble called Kiss (who for several years never had their pictures taken *without* makeup), and the gross antics of Alice Cooper (born Vincent Furnier, a preacher's son), who depended on boa constrictors, gallows, and beheaded chickens to validate his act. Add to the glitz list Ted Nugent, who has appeared onstage clad only in a loincloth, and the New York Dolls, renowned mainly for the fact that lead singer David Johannson is a ringer for Rolling Stone Mick Jagger.

New Wave

In a field of study which, like rock, is full of imprecise terms (what is rock 'n' roll? jazz-rock? soul?), one of the most imprecise is the term "new wave." As much as anything else, the term refers to style of dress and even of haircut. Musically, there are many bands with different styles that might be called new wave.

Consider the following list: the B-52's; the Cars; Devo; the Knack; Men at Work; The Police. What do they all have in common? A heavy debt to their forebears, undoubtedly, to heavy-metal guitar growls, disco's relentless dance beat, reggae, and even primitive rock 'n' roll instrumentals. Often, they also achieve their sound by using new items of equipment and new technology—tuned electronic drums, reverb units, special studio techniques.

Like disco, new wave is intended for dancing. The beat chugs along in a steady eighth-note trot, frequently marked by a stick-tap on closed high-hat cymbals. Vocal phrases are usually short, with instrumentals filling the gaps. New wave has a visual side as well, as can be seen from Devo's upside-down-flowerpot headgear, or the garage band dress of groups like the Cars.

Two foreign groups, The Police (from England) and Men at Work (from Australia) are notable for their musical quality. Both bands are capable of creating bad music when they make the effort, but are fundamentally solid units with strong rhythmic drive and a flair for creating expressive songs. The Police show more reggae influence than most, and some of their song lyrics have a haunting, alienated poetry unusual in Top-Forty bands.

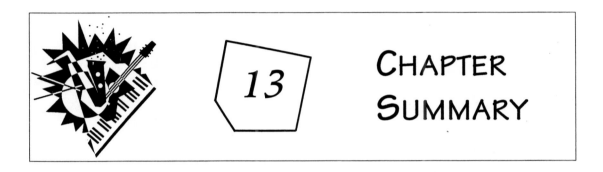

13 CHAPTER SUMMARY

There are hints that, as John Lydon claims, rock is beginning to run out of steam. It's much too early to hold a funeral, but there are signs of decay in the House of Rock 'n' Roll. In some ways, rock has returned to its own first principles: dance, have fun, shock your parents, forget your problems. That, at least, was the message of disco— but then, disco didn't last that long. Reggae was big in Jamaica, but never really caught on in the States. Punk rock also did poorly on this side of the Atlantic, though it had a vogue in Great Britain. There has been a steady market for heavy metal bands for some time, both here and abroad. From time to time, a heavy metal group will turn out a song that does well on the pop charts, too. But the glitz and flash groups burn out quickly. After all, when you buy a record, you can't see the funny or freaky costumes; and many of those bands just can't make it on music alone. Off to MTV, guys.

That leaves the ambiguous new wave bands. Some are quite good, and will probably become established in pop music much as Yes, Led Zeppelin, or the Rolling Stones have. We can't tell what sorts of groups will be the pop music leaders of the future. We can say for sure that the pop music of the year 2020 will be quite different from what is popular today. However, one thing seems certain—it ought to be interesting.

Suggested Projects

1. One of the modern buzzwords, in popular psychology and in rock, is "alienation," meaning "withdrawn, indifferent, estranged." Do you think that modern rock describes alienation in its words or music? If so, how does it do this? Can you think of groups whose music sounds more alienated than most? What does this indicate about the groups or their fans? Write an essay on your thoughts about alienation in rock.

2. "Be Good, Johnny" is a song by Men at Work that has to do with parents nagging their teenage son. In the 1950s, a group called the Drifters recorded a song called "Yackety Yak (Don't Talk Back)," which addressed the same eternal theme. Can you think of other songs that deal with the stresses of teenage life? List and describe the themes of as many as you can find. Be sure to name performers, and include information on record labels and numbers.

14 THE MTV GENERATION

As the styles of rock proliferated like rabbits from the late 1960s on, new musical mixes and technological advances played an increasing role in the development of the broad channel of music lumped together under the title of "rock." Interesting tensions grew between the sophisticates (art rock, jazz-rock) and the fundamentalists (punk rock, rock revival) over how slick or how basic the music should become. Meanwhile, everyone from speed-metal headbangers to "gangsta" rappers exploited the ever more sophisticated technical resources available to them.

Rap

Gonna stay in school 'cause I ain't no fool,

And the one with education is the one that's gonna rule.

So I'll get my diploma, head for college;

Only way to change is to get more knowledge.

Improvising rhymed couplets is a popular and valued pastime in many African societies. The improviser often aims pointed jibes at political officials, to the delight of listeners. Skill at making up such rhymes is considered a mark of cleverness. The same talent is valued in certain other societies of the world—for example, the Dayak peoples of New Guinea.

This glib, fast-talking wit is not unknown in European and American circles, either. Even such an operatic chestnut as Rossini's "Largo al Factotum" from *The Barber of Seville* illustrates the point, as does Gilbert and Sullivan's "When I Was a Lad" from *H.M.S. Pinafore,* among many such "patter songs." Harold Hill's wonderful scam, "Pool," from *The Music Man,* even does away with melody and becomes a chant.

None of these are rap, but they help to put rap into the context of a genre of expression with a long and varied history. Rap has folk roots, for no one person invented it, and it is far from clear just when and where it originated. As a rock phenomenon, it first emerges in the Bronx, New York City, in the 1970s, as one aspect of hip-hop, a lifestyle that also included break-dancing and graffiti art in inner cities.

Disk jockey Kool Herc, a Jamaican immigrant, introduced rap to the New York audience in the late 1970s, beginning with "Rapper's Delight" by the Sugar Hill Gang. This was soon followed by Kurtis Blow and by Grandmaster Flash and the Furious Five. Most recordings were accompanied by live bands, but some took excerpts from other recordings by different performers and arranged these clips into a background collage over which the performers rapped. The texts of many rap songs were largely boasting and trivial, and it seemed that rap was one more fad that would blend into pop music as just another style.

Then new groups, made up of what reviewer Alan Light calls "middle-class rappers approach[ing] the ghetto itself as an outlaw fantasy," seized the public's attention. Performers and groups such as L.L. Cool J, Ice-T, and Public Enemy featured hostile, antisocial raps disparaging women and urging violence. These drew a firestorm of protest from across the nation. Sister Souljah even managed fifteen minutes of fame during the 1992 presidential race. The kids (and others) had finally outraged their tolerant parents in a big way. Prominent black ministers, black-music television channels, and even the NAACP came forth with criticisms of "gangsta rap" as painting an ugly and distorted picture of black America. Rapper Queen Latifah's work protests the often sexually denigrating works of gangsta rappers.

The flap over rap obscured the less offensive work of people like M.C. Hammer, DJ Jazzy Jeff and the Fresh Prince, and white rapper Vanilla Ice. Rap has long had two main styles, "house" or party rap and the more aggressive political rap. Meanwhile, the production of rap songs became vastly more sophisticated. Rather than recording riffs from other songs on tape and overlayering the rap on them, modern rappers use computer-like sampling technology to provide the background clips. What lies ahead for rap? No one knows, so stay tuned.

Music Television

Miss Teen Dream has a problem in the form of a geeky-looking guy in a black bowler hat. She isn't remotely interested in him, but her efforts to ignore him make him more determined, and more obnoxious, than ever. She twists her lipstick tube, and out pops his face. She swats at an insect with his head on its front. Most girls have known a pest who seems to show up everywhere like this, in this mini-drama played out in the Cars' "You Might Think" on MTV. It's only one of the four-minute fantasies available day and night on television sets throughout the nation, wherever cable service is available.

History

The idea of filming rock performances occurred early in the evolution of rock. After all, such performances depend at least as much on visual elements as on musical for their effect. Elvis's rockabilly songs played well on jukeboxes, but what really got the attention (and the parental disapproval) were the gyrations of his hips. Film and videotape clips appeared as short specials on programs like *American Bandstand*, in between the long sequences of teens writhing to recordings. The British did much more with rock videos than the Americans in the earlier years, but finally the United States found the right mix of technical ingenuity and commercial organization.

Music Television (MTV) began in the early 1970s, at first broadcasting only a few hours per day, but gradually increasing to full programming. What made it economically possible was the fact that the tapes were provided by the record companies free of charge, as commercials for their products. This meant that the organizers of the MTV network could get financial backing for their project. From the beginning, the network aimed at the fourteen- to thirty-five-year-old market as the people who would be likely to buy records they had seen performed on MTV. The network's success was phenomenal; within two years, MTV was carried by 1,775 cable operators nationwide.

Because of their early lead in producing rock videos, British groups provided much of the content of early MTV shows, and groups such as Duran Duran and Men at Work were mainly introduced to American audiences on MTV. In the early years, white groups predominated on MTV, since, as the stations reasoned, black groups produced rhythm-and-blues or disco, and not rock 'n' roll. The impasse was broken with Michael Jackson's productions of "Thriller" and "Billy Jean." Whatever it was called, the audiences demanded more of it, and the color barrier in MTV was broken for good.

It was not long before other channels featured rock videos. Ted Turner's WTBS began its six hours of "Night Tracks" on Friday and Saturday nights in 1983. Not long after, the USA Network ran "Night Flight" and "1990," and NBC featured its "Friday Night Videos," a ninety-minute anthology, weekly. The term "MTV" now often refers to the whole field of music videos, much as the term "Kleenex" is used to represent all disposable paper tissues.

As there was no established form for music videos, the field was ripe for experimentation. Many film companies turned out slick, sophisticated four-minute mini-dramas using the latest avant-garde techniques, as there was no prejudice against trying any new idea in the medium. Of course, many of the programs were the sort of hack work that always happens when an entertainment medium needs lots of filler in a short time. The eventual result of such patronage, however, was that the best of the rock videos have had a major influence on film techniques in other fields as well. Many of the full-length films of the late 1980s and 1990s incorporated techniques pioneered in the rock video production studio.

Production

MTV now programs rock videos twenty-four hours a day, seven days a week. Programs are typically taped a full day before they appear on air. Once a week or so a team views the videos that have come in during the previous week and selects the ones that will be included in the new week's programming. Network schedulers seldom worry about censoring the tapes, leaving that to the producing companies. "We have to be careful about violence and frontal nudity," Les Garland of MTV says. "Other than that, it isn't too much of a problem." In the 1990s, the program format enlarged to include "Yo! MTV Raps," short news spots, and special programming such as a group of videos of single performers collectively called the "Most Eligible Bachelor" feature.

Broadcasters pay fees to both ASCAP and BMI, the two licensing agencies that represent composers' and performers' rights to their products. Advertisers pay handsomely to run their commercials, providing the money to keep the business thriving. Record companies find that music videos yield large increases in record sales.

Each video runs four or five minutes, and each provides a strong emotional "hook" to enhance a sometimes obscure story line. Some videos are lavish, expensive productions with highly sophisticated effects. Michael Bolton's "Said I Loved You . . . But I Lied" alternates shots of Bolton singing on a plateau in a desert location (emotional dessication?) with pictures of fire, stallions galloping by, and women in various ecstatic states. The story of the text is thus underlined by the visual images, which have no coherent story of their own. Gin Blossoms' "Found Out About You" is set in a studio, with strobe lights flashing as women stroll past, alternating with cuts of other scenes. The twangy guitars and 1960s-mellow voices are supported by a strong drumbeat. George Michael and Queen's "Somebody to Love" is a 1950s-style, gospel-flavored rock 'n' roll piece with a big band, a large vocal group, and a pseudo-concert setting.

Other videos cost less but are not necessarily less effective. "As Long As I Can Dream" by Expose tells a pretty story of boy-meets-girl in simple terms. Ace of Base use a lot of black-and-white images in "All That She Wants," set to a reggae beat with a strong flavor of Men at Work. The images are depressing, as is the story line; all she wants is another baby, and she is shown dressing up and heading out to a singles bar. John Cougar Mellencamp revived the sophomoric "I Saw Mommy Kissin' Santa Claus" in a performance on a stage, with a Cajun spice provided by a fiddle and accordion, and with a cute little tyke whacking the tambourine. This video not only crosses style lines but is also one of the relatively few multiracial videos. One of the most effective low-budget videos is Bryan Adams's "Please Believe Me," a haunting tune sung in a hoarse, rather adolescent voice, its strong message stated in alternating soft and loud phrases. The producer shot the whole video in a studio with the musicians lounging in their chairs and petting a dog. The strong story line counterpointed by the low-key production makes a memorable performance.

Black performers in videos produce strikingly different settings of songs. Some, like Jodeti ("Cry for You") and Boyz II Men ("It's So Hard to Say Goodbye") and even Janet Jackson ("If"), show a strong influence from Motown, with gospel harmonies, mellow arrangements, and tight choreography. Rappers, too, appear on MTV, including some of the more controversial. In "Dre Day," for example, Dr. Dre and Snoop Doggy Dog incorporate an urban setting in a sexually suggestive skit, but all the males in the video wear hard, detached expressions, as if sex was fine but they have no intention of getting emotional about it.

In short, there is a wide variety of offerings in music videos to suit every taste, mature or adolescent, subdued or ostentatious. The marketers aim for this broad spectrum to hold the maximum audience for the maximum time possible. Researchers estimate that the average MTV-watcher spends five or more hours a week watching music videos and the commercials that attend them. Such a market is highly attractive and increasingly influential in American culture. The prospects are for it to become more so in the future.

Two Headliners: Michael Jackson and Madonna

The tall, sticklike figure bounces about the stage in a series of poses so quickly and sharply performed that the eye can scarcely follow them. Then, for long moments, it freezes in a stance, immobile but for the relentless pounding of the right heel to the thunderous beat. The image is of controlled power, incredible skill, an almost arrogant, dominating charisma.

Michael Jackson began separating from the Jackson Five when, at nineteen, he won the role of the Scarecrow in *The Wiz*, a black musical film takeoff on *The Wizard of Oz*. The film brought him to the attention of veteran composer Quincy Jones, who later produced Michael's first solo album, *Off the Wall*, released in 1979. The album sold well, but it was already apparent that his talent required a visual as well as an aural expression. The result was the 1982 production of *Thriller*, a videotape with companion album that became the largest-selling record in history (over forty million copies worldwide). With its companion videos *Beat It* and *Billie Jean*, *Thriller* set new standards for MTV production.

Where does one go from such a pinnacle? The answer, of course, was down. Jackson's popularity had peaked; the inevitable sniping and carping of critics swelled, fueled in part by the performer's own eccentricities. Despite epic sales of succeeding albums—*Bad* sold over twenty million worldwide, and *Dangerous* did nearly as well—Jackson faded as the idol of the young. A nasty flap over child molestation in 1993 tarnished his image and ended his association with the Disney Corporation. For this enormously creative singer/dancer, his celebrated "moonwalk," in which he moves backward while appearing to move forward, became a metaphor for his career at the close of the century.

Jackson's controversial pop-rock career was, if anything, outdone by that of Detroit's Madonna Louise Ciccone, universally known as just Madonna. Like Michael Jackson, Madonna began as a dancer, working briefly with a second-line troupe of New York's Alvin Ailey Dance Company. From that start she drifted into a singing career, abetted by MTV videos and her passing likeness to Marilyn Monroe.

The "Material Girl" tightened her grip on public controversy with her distinctly sexual performance of the song "Like a Virgin" on a 1985 MTV Music Video Awards program while wearing a bridal gown with a belt buckle that read BOY TOY. A subsequent venture into films met with mixed success, climaxed by the role of Breathless Mahoney in *Dick Tracy*. Nonetheless, her unerring talent for self-promotion by flouting conventions led to a 1992 contract with Time/Warner, reputedly for about $60 million, for future music, film, and publishing ventures. "I like to push people's buttons," she once remarked.

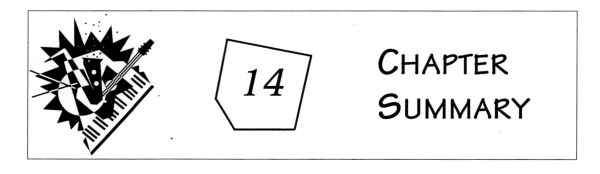

14   CHAPTER SUMMARY

In the decade of the 1970s, black youngsters developed *rap*, and some rappers also made use of cutting-edge recording technology. While much of rap was relatively benign, the sociopathology of *gangsta rap* finally inspired a nationwide wave of disgust and outrage for its celebration of violence and its denigration of women.

Also during the 1970s, music videos provided by record companies were broadcast on special television channels available on cable TV. The industry has grown to a full-time broadcast channel with news and other features as well as rock videos. The videos vary widely in style and expense of production. Most of them are fantasies designed to appeal to the fourteen- to thirty-five-year-old age range. Music videos have pioneered in experimental film techniques, and the results are appearing in feature-length films as well as on MTV. Two of MTV's most successful performers, Michael Jackson and Madonna, have stirred widespread controversy by their actions, with different results.

Suggested Projects

1. Watch an hour of MTV, and write a report on what you see. Look for answers to the following questions:

    a. What style of rock does the video represent?

    b. To what age range would you estimate the video is designed to appeal?

    c. Is the story line clear, or is it mostly emotion-inducing images?

    d. Is the production lavish, or does it seem to be a low-budget video?

    e. Give your assessment of the effectiveness of each video.

    f. What sorts of products are advertised?

2. Create your own rap performance. Write out the text (maybe with the collaboration of friends); tape the result; then tape clips from other recordings for background. If you can get a synthesizer and sample the clips, it will save some effort on your part. Overdub the tapes (electronically, if possible) to produce the end result.

CODA

The *History of Rock Music* has traced the evolution of rock 'n' roll from its roots in black and white American folk and popular music through its many forms to the present. It has been a long and often fascinating journey, and each chapter has told us a lot about the people and the time period in which it was set. We have ventured from the simplistic three-chord rock 'n' roll of Bill Haley to the complex tone poems of Yes, and from the sly double-entendres of Fats Domino ("Blueberry Hill") to the blunt four-letter obscenities of the Sex Pistols. The cast of characters has been huge, but many, many more might have been mentioned.

The history of rock parallels the history of an unprecedented revolution, a churning and reordering of society as profound as the French and Russian revolutions, but with much less bloodshed and destruction. It is difficult for one who has not lived through them to appreciate the social changes in the United States and Western Europe since 1953. That was the year that *Playboy* magazine was born. That year marked the end of the Korean "police action" (and the beginning, one supposes, of the scripting of *M*A*S*H*). Vietnam was French; Angola was Portuguese; Zaire was the Belgian Congo. The United States was run by a white, male establishment that was just beginning to become uncomfortable with inequities of race and gender. In the South, black people rode in the backs of buses and had separate schools. In the North, the racial prejudice was more subtle, but more stubborn.

History records no parallels of a society being able to transform itself so drastically with so little turmoil and violence. True enough, we didn't lack for either turmoil or violence—assassinations of important public figures, riots, bombings by radical student groups, protest marches by hundreds of thousands of people. Consider the following facts, though: The French Revolution lasted for almost a decade, slaughtered tens of thousands, and replaced a king with an emperor; and in Russia, the murders ran into the millions, the turmoil stretched from 1917 to the late 1930s, and in the end, an absolutist csar was replaced by a totalitarian party chairman.

Compared with those two famous revolutions, America's social transformation has been both efficient and benign. At the center of this process of change, rock in its various forms has mobilized the attitudes, and at times the actions, of the young. Born of a fusion of white country and black blues, rock created a brash, strutting accompaniment to the forward march of civil rights. Shaped by the sentiments of people who opposed the Vietnam War, rock gave words and songs to the feelings of the protestors. For good or ill, rock has shaped the thoughts and actions, the dress and lifestyle of nearly two generations—not only here in America, but in Siberia and Malaya and Nigeria and Japan and India as well. Think of it: perhaps the only thing in the world that people of all races, religions, and ideologies agree on is—rock 'n' roll.

What of the future? It's possible only to guess, of course. Rock is showing signs of decay, but it isn't apparent what new kind of music might take its place. Country music is a possible successor; it's too soon to tell. Some kinds of rock—art rock, perhaps heavy metal, very likely some descendant of Motown or the Philadelphia Sound—will probably continue, with sizeable groups of fans, whatever form pop music takes. Very likely some of the elements of rock will increasingly influence various art-music composers, especially the younger ones who have grown up with rock and understand fully its possibilities. After all, that's what happened with jazz.

At any rate, rock has already had a vigorous and colorful history, one that has been sketched in this text. The key word here is "sketched." You may have been disappointed not to have seen your favorite performer or group mentioned here. Lots of important personalities and bands have been omitted for reasons of space. There are so very many names in rock that it would take an encyclopedia to cover them all. This book has attempted to trace the major lines of development in rock, and to mention representative personalities and groups in each category. It is hoped that you, the reader, will make allowances for the omissions and benefit from the overview the text has provided. Keep listening—the story isn't over yet.

GLOSSARY

Art rock—A style of rock, evolving since the late 1960s, which uses characteristics of Western and non-Western classical music. Art rock is discussed in Chapter 11.

Art song—A musical setting of poetry. In the settings of Franz Schubert and Johannes Brahms, the singer is accompanied by a piano.

ASCAP—American Society of Composers, Authors, and Publishers. This agency helps enforce the legal rights of creative artists to control and to benefit from their creative work.

Atonal—Having no tonal center, no "home tone." Much twentieth-century art music is atonal.

BMI—Broadcast Music, Inc. This agency serves the same purpose as ASCAP. The main distinction is that BMI more commonly represents popular-music composers and performers.

Ballad—Any song that tells a story over several verses with a repeated melody.

Bluegrass—A modern name for country or hillbilly music, as distinct from country and western. White music derived from European folk music and featuring guitars, fiddles, and string bass.

Blues—A black American song form that apparently began after the Civil War as a folk tradition. It is described in detail in Chapter 3.

Blues changes—The chord progression typically associated with a blues.

Cadenza—A lengthy, free improvisation designed to show the skill of an instrumental performer. It is played without steady beat or meter.

Country and western—A variant of bluegrass, utilizing more composed songs, more amplified instruments, drums, and usually given slicker production. It is described in Chapter 4.

Folk-rock—A soft-rock idiom borrowing material and style from the folk-song traditions of various nations, especially England and the United States. It is described in Chapter 8.

Funky—Originally, this word meant "smelly." An earthy, strong, rhythmic black musical style with a gospel feel.

Gamelan—An Indonesian percussion orchestra, very sonorous and often quite exciting.

Gospel—Black church-music tradition that stresses call-and-response, strong rhythm, and the use of primary chords.

Hillbilly music—The name applied to white folk-based country music before the Second World War. It was an ancestor of country and western music, and is described in Chapter 4.

Improvisation—Music that is made up, based on certain principles of chord or scale, on the spur of the moment. It is contrasted with written or even worked-out music.

Motown—A very influential style of black popular music that originated in Detroit, the Motor City. It is discussed in Chapter 10.

Oud—An Arabian stringed instrument known in the West as a lute.

Polyphony—Music that has a texture of two or more melodies occurring at the same time.

Rhythm-and-blues—A citified derivative of black folk blues, usually performed by several instruments and a singer, and serving as a direct ancestor of rock 'n' roll. It is discussed in Chapter 3.

Rhythm cycle—A repeating rhythm pattern, from three to as many as twenty-eight beats, that is often found in Arab or East Indian music. Unlike a meter, the rhythm cycle often contains subgroupings of several beats.

Riff—A repeating rhythmic and melodic idea used in a song. A riff usually lasts for only one or two verses, and is often the background to a melody.

Sansa—An African instrument with several tuned metal prongs that are plucked with the thumbs. It is also known as a *kalimba*, *lukembi*, *mbira*, or thumb piano.

Soul—Black musical style that emphasized its growing out of the black experience. It is associated with genuine feelings, as opposed to put-on posturings.

Techno-rock—A term used to disparage rock performers or groups who get carried away with showing off musical technique at the expense of being expressive.

BIBLIOGRAPHY

Thousands of books about rock are in print, the vast majority of them concerning individual performers or groups. For an overview of the field from its beginnings, the following works may be of most use. All take a rather purist view of what rock is, and none of them list, for example, Spyro Gyra, although some include Dolly Parton. The *Harmony Encyclopedia* contains occasional useful "genealogy charts" showing the relationships between various groups at various times.

Clifford, Mike (ed.). *Harmony Encyclopedia of Rock*. New York: Harmony Books, 1992.

Decurtis, Anthony, and James Henke, eds. *Rolling Stone Illustrated Encyclopedia of Rock & Roll*. New York: Random House, 1992.

Heatley, Michael, ed. *The Ultimate Encyclopedia of Rock*. New York: Harper Perennial, 1993.

Other works that may be of some interest include the following:

Frith, Simon, and Andrew Goodwin, eds. *On Record: Rock, Pop, and the Written Word*. New York: Pantheon Books, 1990. The section on "The Music Business" is quite useful.

Stambler, Irwin. *The Encyclopedia of Pop, Rock, and Soul*. New York: St. Martin's Press, 1989. Lots of detail on the persons and groups covered, but its criteria are baffling; it includes Barbra Streisand and omits Spyro Gyra, for example.

Ward, Ed, Geoffrey Stokes, and Ken Tucker. *Rock of Ages: The Rolling Stone History of Rock & Roll*. New York: Rolling Stone Press/Summit Books, 1986. Some of the language is quite crude.

INDEX

A

A & M Records, 85
AC/DC, 1, 86
Ace of Base, 92
acid, 59. *See also* LSD.
acid rock, 55, 85
    arrival of, 60
    characteristics of, 61
    drug culture of, 62
    fading of, 61
acoustic instruments, 60, 84
Acuff, Roy, 27
adolescents
    rock and, 33
    MTV and, 94
Adams, Bryan, 92
Aeolian mode, 55
Aerosmith, 86
Africa, musical traditions of, 15
African music
    disco and, 83
    improvised rhymed couplets in, 89
Alcatraz, 45
Alvin Ailey Dance Company, 94
American Bandstand, 91
American Grafitti, 46
American Indian Movement, 52
American Society of Composers, Authors, and
    publishers. *See* ASCAP.
Ammons, Albert, 8

amplification, electrical , 27 , 32
    in acid rock, 61
Anderson, Ian, 74
Anderson, Jon, 72, 73
Andrews Sisters, the, 26, 35
Angola, 97
Animals, the, 41
anti-culture, punk and, 85
antisocial raps, 90
antiwar sentiment, musical, 52, 54
Apocalypse, 74
Apollo Theater, 65
Appalachian Mountains, 22, 24
Armstrong, Louis, 65
Arnold, Eddie, 27
art music, 76
art rock, 42, 71, 89. *See also* symphonic rock.
    bands, 72
    mini-symphony in, 73
    origins of, 74
ASCAP (American Society of Composers, Authors,
    and Publishers), 27, 92
    composers and, 26
Asia, 75
Atlantic Records, 66
atonal chord progression, 75
Australia, 87
Autry, Gene, 25, 26, 27, 28, 38, 66

B

Babes In Toyland, 5

"Baby, You're a Rich Man," 43

background music, 52

Bach, Johann Sebastian, 71

Bad, 93

Bad Company, 86

Baez, Joan, 53, 54, 55

ballads , 8 , 14, 23 , 28

   Anglo-American, 22, 24

   crooners of, 25

   themes of, 22

banjo, 4, 22, 23, 24, 27, 41

   in folk music, 54

Barber of Seville, 89

Barn Dance, 25, 26

Bartók, Béla, 74

bass, 27

   in heavy metal, 85

Beach Boys, the, 54, 60

   careful production of, 48

   counterpoint of, 46

   harmonization of, 46

   overdubbing used by, 46–47

beat

   of rock 'n' roll, 34, 35

   swing, 35

Beat Generation, 37

Beat It, 93

Beatles, the, 34, 38-40, 41, 42-43, 47, 53, 55, 71, 72

   Beatlemania and, 38

   electronic distortions of, 40

   musical maturing of, 40

   symphony orchestra used by, 40

Bee Gees, the, 41

Beethoven, Ludwig van, 71, 83

B-48's, the, 86

Belafonte, Harry, 84

Belgian Congo, 97

Benatar, Pat, 86

Berkeley, student radicals at, 61

Berlin airlift, 32

Berlin, Irving, 4, 5

Berlioz, Hector, 59

Bernstein, Leonard, 72

Berry, Chuck, 18, 34, 37

Berry, Jan, 46, 47. *See also* Beach Boys.

   car wreck of, 48

Beverly Hills 90210, 45

Big Brother and the Holding Company, 60, 61

Big Daddy Donahue, 60. *See also* Donahue, Tom.

Bill Haley and the Comets, 31

Billboard magazine, 27, 38

Billie Jean, 93

Bitches Brew, 80

Black Moses, 66

Black Sabbath, 85, 86

black-face makeup, 4

Bland, Bobby Blue, 34

Bland, James, 4

Blind Lemon Jefferson, 65

Blood, Sweat, and Tears, 80, 81

Bloomfield, Mike, 62

blue notes, 17, 33

Blue Öyster Cult, 86

blue yodel, 24

bluegrass, 24, 55

   and rock, 33

blues, 8, 15-16, 19, 65, 66

   as American style, 17

   chord progression, 47

   country, 18

      instruments used with, 18

   in disco, 83

   emotion of, 54

   form, 33

   in funky jazz, 79

   harmonic conventions in, 16

   migration of, 26

   progression, 16

   scale, 17

BMI (Broadcast Music, Inc.), 26, 27, 92

Bo Diddley, 34

Bob Marley and the Wailers, 84

body music, 31, 32, 83. *See also* dance music.
  disinterest in, 55
Boggs, Dock, 24
Bolton, Michael, 92
Bonner, M.J. , 25
boogie-woogie, 8
Booker T and the MG's, 35, 66
bop, 79, 81
Boyz II Men, 93
break-dancing, 90
Broadcast Music, Inc. *See* BMI.
Broadway musicals, 8
Brothers Gibb, the. *See* Bee Gees.
Brown, Clifford, 79
Brown, James, 34, 65
Bruford, Bill, 73, 75
Brunswick, 23
Butterfield Blues Band, 62
Byrds, the, 55

C

California
  lifestyle of southern, 45
  music, 55
  as music center, 48
  musical groups, 54
California Sound, the, 42, 46, 47
call-and-response singing, 15, 18, 19
Calloway, Cab, 7
calypso, 84
Camp Curry, 45
Candix Records, 46
Cannon, Freddie, 34
Cannon, Hughie, 4
Cannonball Adderly, 80
canticle, 75
Capitol Records, 46
Caribbean music, 80, 84
Carl and the Passions, 45
Carnaval, 82
Carnegie Hall, 38

Carousel, 6
Cars, the, 86, 87, 90
Carter Family, the 24, 53
Carter, Maybelle, 23
Casa Loma Orchestra, 7
"Cashaça," 82
Casino Royale, 41
Cavemen, the, 37, 38
celesta, 8
censorship, 92
Chad and Jeremy, 41
Chad Mitchell Trio, 54
chanting, 89
Charles, Ray, 18, 65
Checker, Chubby, 18, 83
Cherry, Don, 79
Chicago, 80, 81
Chicago Transit Authority. *See* Chicago.
Child ballads, 52, 53
Chocolate Chip, 66
Christy Minstrels, 54
Ciccone, Madonna Louise. *See* Madonna.
civil rights, 60
Civil War, 4, 15
Clapton, Eric, 41
clarinet, 65
Clark, Petula, 41, 42
Clarke, Stanley, 80
Clash, The, 85
classical music, Indian, 39, 55, 61
Clockwork Orange, A, 84
Close Encounters, 51
"Close to the Edge," 77
Clyde, Jeremy, 41
Coasters, the, 34
Cobham, John, 80
Cochran, Eddie, 34
coffeehouses, 53-54
  folk music and, 52
Cohan, George M., 4, 5
Coleman, Ornette, 79

Collins, Judy, 54

Collins, Phil, 72

Columbia, 23

cool jazz, 79, 80, 81

Cooper, Alice, 86

Copland, Aaron, 72

Corea, Chick, 80, 81

Costello, Elvis, 73

Count Basie, 7 , 11-12, 32

counterpoint, 46, 74

country and western, 25, 26, 28

   musicians, 27

   singers, and early rock, 31

Country Joe and the Fish, 60

Country Joe MacDonald, 61

country music, 23, 26

    and gospel style, 66

    performers, 24

Crack the Sky, 75

Cream, 41

Cropper, Steve, 66

Crosby, Bing, 7, 27, 53

Crosby, David, 55

crystal sets, 6

cymbals, high-hat, 86

D

Dalhart, Vernon, 24

dance music, 18, 22. *See also* body music.

dancing, rock 'n' roll and, 32

Dangerous, 93

Daniels, Charlie, 75

Dave Brubeck Quartet, 79

Dave Clark Five, 40, 41

Davis, Jimmie, 27

Davis, Miles, 73, 74, 79, 80, 81

Day, Doris, 8

Dayak peoples, 89

DC 5. *See* Dave Clark Five.

Death Valley, 45

Deep Purple, 85, 86

Def Leppard, 85

destructo-rock, 41

Detroit, Michigan, 67

Devo, 86, 87

Diana Ross and the Supremes, 67

Dick Tracy, 94

diMeola, Al, 80

disco, 68, 83

   demise of, 84

   message of, 87

   new wave and, 86

   style of, 83

discotheque, 83-84

Disney Corporation, 93

distortion

   electronic, 40, 62

   feedback, in heavy metal, 85

Dixie Dregs, 75

Dixie Mountaineers, 24

Dixieland jazz, 52

Dock Boggs, 24

Dodds, Johnny, 65

DJ Jazzy Jeff and the Fresh Prince, 90

"Doggin' Around," 11-12

Domino, Fats, 19, 73, 83

   double entendres of, 34, 97

Donahue, Tom, 60

Donovan, 53, 56

Dorian mode, 39, 55

Dorsey, Tommy, 7, 8, 31, 32

Downs, Geoff, 75

Dozier, Lamont, 67

Dr. Dre, 93

"Drag City," 47

Dregs, the, 75

Dregs of the Earth, 75

Drifters, the, 34

drug(s)

   culture, of San Franciso, 62

   experimentation, in music, 54

   music, 60. *See also* San Francisco Sound.

use, 55

    young people and, 59

drums, 28, 33

    in folk-rock, 54

    in heavy metal, 85

    in speed metal, 86

    tuned electric, 86

dulcimer, 22

    in folk music, 54

Dunn, Donald "Duck," 66

Duran Duran, 91

Dust Bowl, 23

Dvořák, Antonín, 72

Dylan, Bob, 4, 53, 54, 56

E

Earth, Wind, and Fire, 68, 80, 84

Eastman Rochester School of Music, 80

"Eleanor Rigby," 39, 53

electronic music, 75, 76

Ellington, Duke, 7, 32

ELP (Emerson, Lake, and Palmer), 72, 73, 75

Emerson, Keith, 72

Emerson, Lake, and Palmer (ELP), 71. *See also* ELP.

EMI, 84-85

Emmett, Dan, 4

England, 87

    art rock and, 74, 76

    reggae in, 84

    rock videos and, 91

entertainment

    pre-electronic, 51

    songs, 13, 14

Epstein, Brian, 38

Eric Burdon and the New Animals, 41

Evans, Gil, 79

Everly Brothers, 35

Every Good Boy Deserves Favour, 72

Expose, 92

F

Falcons, the, 34

feedback distortion, 85

Ferguson, Maynard, 80

fiddle, 22, 23, 24, 26, 27

    soloists, 25

Fillmore Ballroom, 61

Fish, 61

Final Solution, 60

Flack, Roberta, 66

Flamingoes, 34

Foley, Red, 27

folk music, 15, 23, 60

    American, 21

    black, 13, 68

    Anglo-Irish, 74

    authentic styles of, 23

    English and West European style, 28

    Euro-American, interest in, 55

    pop tunes and, 4

    revival of, 52

    roots, of rap, 90

    style, 53

    white, 14

folk-rock, 52, 54

    emotional commitment and, 56

    expression in, 56

folk singers, 52

    influence of black music and, 54

folk songs

    authentic, 53

    British, and the Beatles, 39

Fortune Teller, The, 5

Foster, Stephen, 4

Four Freshmen, the, 46, 54

Four Tops, the, 67

Fragile, 73

Franklin, Aretha, 18, 66

free jazz, 79

Free Speech Movement, 52

Freiberg, David, 61

French horns, 8
  swing and, 32
French Revolution, 97
Friml, Rudolph, 6
Fripp, Robert, 73
Fruit Jar Drinkers, the, 25
funk, 68
  in jazz, 79
Funkadelic, 68
Furnier, Vincent. *See* Cooper, Alice.
fusion, 80, 81

G

Gabriel, Peter, 72
Gallo wines, 45
Gamble, Ken, 67
gamelan music, 74
gangsta rap, 89
  criticisms of, 90
  sociopathology of, 94
Gaye, Marvin, 67
Genesis, 72
Gennett, 23
Gentle Giant, 72
Germany, 32
Getz, Stan, 79
  heroin use and, 59
Gid Tanner and His Skillet Lickers, 24. *See also*
  Tanner, Gideon.
Gilbert and Sullivan, 89
Gillespie, Dizzy, 79
Gilliland, Henry, 23
Gilmer, Jimmy, 34
Girl from Utah The, 5
Gin Blossoms, 92
Gladys Knight and the Pips, 67
Glenn Miller Orchestra, 8, 10–11
glitz rock, 55, 86, 87
Golden Gate Bridge, 45
Gong, 74, 75
Goodman, Benny, 7, 8, 32

Gordy, 67
Gordy, Berry, 67
gospel, 19, 52. *See also* religious songs, spirituals.
  harmonies in, 18
  country style and, 66
  songs, 18, 65
graffiti art, 90
Grand Funk Railroad, 86
Grand Ole Opry, 25
Grandmaster Flash and the Furious Five, 90
Grateful Dead, 48, 60, 62
Grauman's Chinese Theater, 45
Great Depression, 7, 53
Great Society, 60, 61
guitar, 22, 23, 24, 28, 54, 60
  amplification, 2, 27
  acoustic, in folk music, 54
  Hawaiian steel, 26, 27, 28
  in heavy metal, 86
    technique, 85
Gully Jumpers, 25
Guthrie, Woody, 53

H

Haley, Bill, 37. *See also* Bill Haley and the Comets.
  simplistic rock 'n' roll of, 97
Half Dome, 45
Halligan, Dick, 80
Hammerstein, Oscar, 6
Hancock, Herbie, 73, 80, 81
Handy, William C., 4
hard-bop regression, 79
harmonica, 60
harmonization, 17, 46
harmony, 45, 46
  chromatic, 5
  folk, 55
    -tune, of rock, 35
  gospel, 18
  of rock 'n' roll, 34
Harrison, George, 38, 39

Hart, Lorenz, 6
Hatch, Tony, 41
Hayes, Isaac, 66
HDH. *See* Dozier, Lamont, Holland, Brian, and
   Holland, Eddie.
head-banging, 86
heavy metal, 63, 85-86, 87
Hell's Angels, 40
Hendrix, Jimi, 41, 42, 61, 63, 85
   barbiturate overdose of, 62
Herbert, Victor, 5
Herman's Hermits, 41
Hi Los, 46
Hill, Harold, 89
hillbilly music, 2, 22–23, 24, 25, 26, 28
   composers and performers, 27
Hindu
   classical music, 74
   musical systems, 71
   philosophy, 41
Hines, Earl, 8
hip-hop, 90
hippies, 60
H.M.S. Pinafore, 89
Holdsworth, Alan, 75
Holland, Brian, 67
Holland, Eddie, 67
Hollies, the, 41, 42
Holly, Buddy, 34, 37, 41
Holst, Gustav Theodore, 71
Hot Buttered Soul, 66
hot-rod songs, 46, 47
house rap, 90
Howard, Joe, 4
Howe, Steve, 72, 75
Huff, Leon, 67
hyper-amplification, 85

I

Ice-T, 90
Impressions, the, 34

improvisation, 19
   in bop, 79
   melodic variation by, 15
Incredible String Band, 41
India
   classical music of, 39, 55, 61
   music of, 80
   philosophy of, 80
Ink Spots, the, 35
instrumental music, 25
instrumentation
   in gospel music, 18
   swing, 32
instruments, 19
   early dance music and, 28
   rhythm, in swing, 32
Irish jigs, 22
Iron Maiden, 85
Isaac Hayes Movement, The, 66
Islamic music, 71
Isley Brothers, 62, 67
Ives, Burl, 53

J

Jackson, Al, 66
Jackson Five, 67 , 93
Jackson, Janet, 93
Jackson, Michael, 2, 67, 94
   career problems of, 93
   MTV and, 91
Jagger, Mick, 40, 86
Jamaica, 84
   reggae in, 87
Japan, 32
Jardine, Al, 45, 46
jazz, 2, 7 , 8, 79
   avant-garde, 41, 73
   big-band, 80
   cool, 79, 80, 81
   instruments used in, 18
   origins of, 18

personalities, drug use and, 59
jazz-rock, 80, 81, 89
jazz-rock fusion. *See* fusion.
Jefferson Airplane, 48, 60, 62. *See also* Jefferson
   Starship.
Jefferson Starship, 61
Jennings, Waylon, 52
Jethro Tull, 74
jigs, 22
Jimi Hendrix Experience, 62
Jobson, Eddie, 75
Jodeti, 93
Johannson, David, 86
John, Elton, 41
Johnson, Pete, 8
Jones, Booker T. *See* Booker T and the MG's.
Jones, Quincy, 93
Jones, Tom, 41
Joplin, Janis, 53, 61, 62
Journey into the Secret Life of Plants, 71
Judas Priest, 85
jukeboxes, 7, 91
   country music on, 28

K

Kansas, 75
Kazee, Buell, 23, 24
Kenny and the Cadets, 45
Kenton, Stan, 80
Kern, Jerome, 5, 6
Kincaid, Bradley, 23
King and I, The, 6
King, B.B., 53
King Crimson, 73, 75, 80
King Records, 65
Kingston Trio, 54
Kirby, John, 7
Knack, the, 86
Knox, Buddy, 34
Kool Herc, 90
Korean War, 32

end of, 97
koto, 47
Kurtis Blow, 90

L

Lake, Greg, 72, 73
L.A. Law, 45
L.L. Cool J, 90
Lamplighters, the, 35
Lang-Venuti All-Stars, 7
Larks' Tongues in Aspic, 73
LC. *See* Library of Congress.
Led Zeppelin, 85, 87
Leitch, Donovan, 54
Ledbetter, Huddie, 53
Lennon, John, 38, 39
   assassination of, 40
Lewis, Mead Lux, 8
Library of Congress (LC), 53
Light, Alan, 90
Lipsius, Fred, 80
Little Johnny Jones, 5
Little Richard, 19, 34, 62
Liverpool, England, 37, 38
Lizard, 73
London, England, 84
"Long Dark Road," 42
Lord of the Flies, 72
Los Angeles, California, 45
   speed metal of, 86
Louis Armstrong Hot Five, 7
Love, Mike, 46
LSD (lysergic acid diethylamide), 59–60, 61. *See
   also* acid rock.
   Tom Donahue and, 60
lullabies, 14
Lydon, John, 84–85, 87. *See also* Rotten, Johnny.
lyrics, of popular music, 3. *See also* texts.
   symbolist, 73

M

Ma Rainey, 65

McCartney, Paul, 38, 39

McGuinn, Roger, 55

McLaren, Malcolm, `84

McLaughlin, John, 55, 74, 80

Macon, Uncle Dave, 23, 25

Madonna, 94

madrigal, English, 72

Magma, 74

Mahavishnu Orchestra, 74, 80

"Majestic Dance," 82

Malibu, California, 45

Malherbe, Didier, 74

Mamas and the Papas, 53, 54, 55

mambo, Cuban, 84

mandolin, 24

marijuana, 60

M*A*S*H, 97

M.C. Hammer, 90

Meet the Beatles, 38

Mellencamp, John Cougar, 92

Memphis Group. *See* Booker T and the MG's.

Memphis, Tennessee, 66, 67

Men at Work, 86, 87, 91, 92

Metallica, 86

Michael, George, 92

microphones, 6

Miller, Glenn, 7 , 32

Miller, Steve, 62

minor scale, 17

minstrel show, 4, 8

Miracles, the, 67

Mitchell, Joni, 83

Mixolydian mode, 39, 55

Mlle. Modiste, 5

Moby Grape, 60, 61

modalism, 39

Modern Jazz Quartet, 79

Modernaires, the, 26, 35

Moerlen, Pierre, 74

Monk, Thelonius, 79

Monkees, the, 34

Monroe, Marilyn, 45, 94

Monterey, California, 45

Moody Blues, 72

Moondogs, the, 37

"Moonlight Serenade," 10–11

Moonshiners, the, 37

Moore, Sam. *See* Sam and Dave.

Motor City. *See* Detroit, Michigan.

moshing, 86

Motley Crüe, 86

Motörhead, 85

Motown, 67

    influence on MTV, 93

    sound, 68

mountain music, 24

Mozart, Wolfgang Amadeus, 71, 83

MTV, 51, 87, 90–94

Muir, John, 45

music

    black American, 14

    body, 32

    ethnic, 18

    saturation with, 51

    styles, evolution of, 32

Music Man, The, 89

music videos, 91, 93, 94. *See also* rock video.

    experimentation of, 91

musicals, 5

Mussorgsky, Modest Petrovich, 71

mysticism, Hindu, 74

N

NAACP (National Association for the Advancement of Colored People), 90

Nash, Graham, 55

National Barn Dance, 25

Naughty Marietta, 5

New Christy Minstrels, 54

New Guinea, 89

new wave, 85, 86–87
    bands, 75
New World Symphony, 72
New York Dolls, 86
Nice, The, 72
Night of the Living Dead, 59
nihilism, 84
Nolan, Bob, 26
Noone, Peter, 41
North Carolina Ramblers, 24
"Norwegian Wood," 39
Nugent, Ted, 86

O

O'Brien, Mary Catherine. *See* Springfield, Dusty.
Ochs, Phil, 54
Off the Wall, 93
Okeh, 23
Oklahoma!, 6
Oklahoma Cowboy. *See* Autry, Gene.
opera, rock and, 71
operettas, 4, 5, 8
orchestra, use of, 8
Original Hillbillies, the, 24
Osbourne, Ozzie, 85, 86
ostinato, 8, 74, 80
oud, 41, 42
overdubbing, 46–47

P

Page, Jimmy, 85
Palm Springs, California, 45
Palmer, Carl, 72, 75
Parker, Charlie, 79
    and heroin use, 59
Parliaments, 68
party rap, 90
patter songs, 89
percussion instruments, swing and, 32
performances, live, 51
Periodic Table of Elements, 85

permissiveness, 59
Pet Sounds, 47
Peter, Paul, and Mary, 53, 54
phonograph, 52
    early, 6
Peterson, Ray, 34
Philadelphia International Records, 67
Philadelphia sound, 67, 68
piano, 4, 24
Pictures at an Exhibition, 71, 72
Planets, 71
Playboy magazine, 97
player piano, 6
plutonium, 85
Poitier, Sidney, 41
Police, The, 75, 84, 86-87
political rap, 90
Pollack, Ben, 7
polyphony, 73
Ponty, Jean-Luc, 74
popular music, 3, 52
    drug advocacy and, 61
    lyrics of, 3
    topical, 4
Porter, Cole, 6
Prater, Dave. *See* Sam and Dave.
Premiata Forneria Marconi (PFM), 75
Presley, Elvis, 31, 34, 38, 53, 91
Pride, Charlie, 53
progression, blues, 16-17
Prokofiev, Sergey Sergeyvich, 80
psychedelic effects, 60, 61–63
Public Enemy, 90
Puckett, Riley, 23
punk rock, 85, 87, 89
    frustration and anger of, 84

Q

Quarrymen Skiffle Group, the, 37
Queen, 92
Queen Latifah, 90
Quicksilver Messenger Service, 60, 61

R

radio, 23, 52
  barn dance, 25
  beginnings of, 6–7
  stations, 51
    country music on, 28
Raelettes, the, 65
raga-rock, 55
ragtime, 4, 7 , 8
Rainbow, 85
Rainey, Ma, 65
rap, 89–90, 94. *See also* gansta rap.
  antisocial, 90
  on MTV, 93
RareEarth, 67
Rastafarianism, reggae and, 84
RCA Victor, 23, 24, 25
Reagan, Ronald, 45
record companies
  MTV and, 91
  music videos and, 92
recording, acoustical, 6
recording industry, 23
Red Mill, The, 5
Redding, Otis, 65, 66
reggae, 84
  disco and, 83
  influence, and The Police, 87
  new wave and, 86
religious songs, 13–14. *See also* gospel, spirituals.
Return to Forever, 80, 81, 82
reverb, 85, 86
revolution, rock, 35
Revolver, 47
rhythm, 19
  in gospel music, 18
  instruments, in swing, 32
  of rock, 33
  of rock 'n' roll, 34
rhythm-and-blues, 2, 18, 19, 26, 39, 55
  beat, early rock and, 31

Aretha Franklin and, 66
  Berry Gordy and, 67
  musicians, 27
  rock and, 33
Rich, Buddy, 80
ring shouts, 14
Ritter, Tex, 26, 27
Robertson, Eck, 23
Robinson, Bill Smokey, 67
rockabilly, 46
rock
  as an American expression, 2
  classical music and, 71
  grotesqueness in, 86
  paralleling social changes, 97
  performances, filming, 91
  performers and drugs, 59
  revival, 89
  as revolution, 97–98
  as satire, 39
  synthesis of, with art music, 72
  and Vietnam War, 97
rock 'n' roll, 1, 19, 27, 31, 33, 60
  as American pop-music idiom, 35
  bands, early, 32
  different schools of, 42
  drug use and, 55
  ensembles, 35
  essence of, 2
  primitive, and new wave, 86
  sexual lyrics and, 34
  as worldwide entertainment, 1–2, 97
rock videos, 91-92. *See also* music videos.
rockabilly, 39, 91
Rodeo, 72
Rodgers, James Charles. *See* Rodgers, Jimmie.
Rodgers, Jimmie, 24, 25, 28
Rodgers, Richard, 6
Rogers, Roy, 26, 27, 28
Rogers, Will, 25
Rolling Stones, the, 40, 41, 42, 87

Rollins, Sonny, 79
Romantic Warrior, 82
Rossini, Antonio, 89
Rotten, Johnny, 84-85
royalties, 26
Russian Revolution, 97

S

Sainte-Marie, Buffy, 53, 54, 56
Sam and Dave, 66
San Francisco, California, 59, 61
San Francisco Sound, 60, 61
sansa, 74
Santana, Carlos, 61
sapeh, 1
satanic cults, 86
Satie, Erik, 75, 80
Saturday Night Fever, 83
saxophones, in swing, 32, 33
scale
    blues, 17
    exotic, 76
    minor, 17
School of Music of the University of Miami, 75
Schulman, Derek, 72
Schulman, Phil, 72
Schulman, Ray, 72
Scottish jigs, 22
Sears Roebuck and Montgomery Ward, 23, 26
Seeger, Charles, 53
Seeger, Peggy, 53, 54
Seeger, Pete, 53, 54
Sergeant Pepper's Lonely Hearts Club Band, 40, 47, 71
sex, rock lyrics and, 34
Sex, 84
Sex Pistols, 84–85
    obscenities of, 97
Shadows, the, 34
Shaft, 66
Shankar, Ravi, 39

Shaw, Artie, 31
Shearing, George, 80
sheet music, 6
Shorter, Wayne, 80, 81
Showboat, 5
shuffle dances, 14
Sigma Sound Studios, 67
Sills, Stephen, 55
Silver, Horace, 79
Silver Beatles, the, 38
Simon and Garfunkel, 41, 53, 83
Sinatra, Frank, 31
Sinfonie Fantastique, 59
Sister Souljah, 90
sitar, 39, 40, 41, 42, 47, 71–72
Slaughter, Marion. *See* Dalhart, Vernon.
slavery, 18
slaves, African, 19
    music of, 13
Slick, Grace, 61
Sly and the Family Stone, 68
Slye, Leonard. *See* Rogers, Roy.
Smile, 47
Smiley Smile, 47
Smith, Bessie, 65
Smokey Robinson and the Miracles, 67
Snoop Doggy Dog, 93
solo songs, 22
solos
    expressive, in cool jazz, 79
    guitar, in speed metal, 86
    instrumental, 73
    jazz-style jamming, 80
    simultaneous, 41
Soul, 67
soul music, 65, 68
Sound of Music, The, 6
South Pacific, 6
Soviet Union, 32
Spanish gypsy songs, 65
speed metal, 86, 89

Spence, Skip, 61
Spiderman, 2
spirituals, 14, 18, 19. *See also* gospel, religious songs.
Springfield, Dusty, 41
Spyro Gyra, 80–81, 82
Squire, Chris, 72
Staples Singers, 66
Star Wars, 51
Starless and Bible Black, 73
Starr, Ringo, 38
Stax Records, 66, 67
Steely Dan, 48
Steve Miller Band, 60
Stewart, Jim, 66
Stewart, Sylvester, 68
Stockhausen, Karlheinz, 74
Stoneman, Pop, 23
Strauss, Richard, 71
Stravinsky, Igor, 74
Streets of San Francisco, 45
stride piano, 7–8
string bands, 25
string bass, 26, 27, 28
strobe lights, 61
Stuart, Chad, 41
Sugar Hill Gang, 90
Sullivan, Ed, 38, 40
"Surfin' USA," 46
surfing, 45-46
   music, superficiality of, 48
Sutter, John, 45
swing, 8, 31, 32
   bands, 7, 79
     classic, 32
   era, 7 ,
     end of, 9, 35
     high point of, 8
     harmonic effects in, 35
"Swing Low, Sweet Chariot," 14–15
symphonic rock, 42. *See also* art rock.
syncopation, 4, 15, 73

in gospel music, 18
   of Spyro Gyra, 80
synthesizer, 71

T

Tamla Records, 67
Tanner, Gideon, 23
tarantella, 75
Tatum, Art, 8
technology
   computer-like sampling, used by rappers, 90
   early, 6
   new, 86
techno-rock, 73
Temptations, the, 15
texts. *See also* lyrics.
   of the Beatles, 39
   of popular music, 3
   rap, 90
   rock, 35
   swing, 35
Their Satanic Majesties Request, 40
third-stream music, 71
Thomas, Carla, 66
Thompson, Uncle Jimmy, 25
Three Friends, 72
Thriller, 93
Time/Warner, 94
Tin Pan Alley, 5, 7, 24
Tinsel Town, 45
Tomita, 71
Tommy, 41, 71
tone poems, 71
Torrance, Dean, 46, 47, 48. *See also* the Beach Boys.
Toto, 75
Tournament of Roses, 45
Travolta, John, 83
Trick of the Tail, 72
trombones, swing, 32
trumpets, swing, 32
Tubb, Ernest, 26, 27, 28

Turner, Ted, 91
Turner, Tina, 15, 18
Two for the Show, 75

U

UK, 75
Uncle Dave Macon, 23, 25
Uncle Jimmy Thompson, 25
United States, 97
University of California at Berkeley, 61
unrest, social, 62
uranium, 85
USA Network, 91

V

Valentino, Rudolph, 45
values, traditional, questioning of, 61
van Halen, Eddie, 86
Vanilla Ice, 90
van Zander, Christian, 74
Vicious, Sid, 85
Vietnam, 97
Vietnam War, 60
    protests, folk-rock and, 55
    resurgence of folk music and, 52
    rock and, 98
violins, in disco, 83
VIP, 67
Virgin Records, 85
Vocalion, 23
vocalists, 25
    swing and, 32

W

Wagner, Richard, 71
Waller, Fats, 8
War on Poverty, 52
WBAP, 23, 25
Weather Report, 80, 81
West Side Story, 3, 72

Wetton, John, 75
White, Lenny, 80
Whiteman, Paul, 7
Whitesnakes, 85
Who, the, 41, 71
Wilson, Brian, 45–46, 47, 48
Wilson, Carl, 45–47
Wilson, Dennis, 45-46
Wilson, Teddy, 8
Wilson Pickett and the O'jays, 67
wind instruments, swing, 32, 35
Whiz The, 93
Wizard of Oz, The, 93
WLS, 25, 26
Wonder, Stevie, 67, 71
World Becomes the World, The, 75
words, message of, 55 *See also* lyrics, text.
work songs, 13
World War I, 4
World War II, 5
    and rock 'n' roll music, 28
    and folk-music revival, 52
    migration caused by, 26
    swing and post-, 32
    USO shows and, 8
Wray, Faye, 45
WSM, 25
WTBS, 91

Y

Yes, 72-73, 75, 77, 80, 87
    complex tone poems of, 97
Yosemite Valley, 45
Young, Steve, 45

Z

Zaire, 97
Zawinul, Joe, 80, 81
Zebra, 75
Zimmerman, Bob. *See* Dylan, Bob.